HOME DESIGN WORKBOOKS

ONE-ROOM LIVING

LIVING

HOME DESIGN WORKBOOKS
ONE-ROOM LIVING

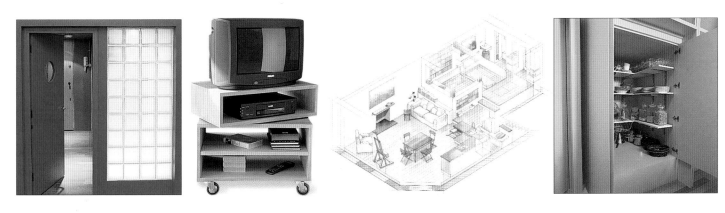

SYLVIA KATZ

DK PUBLISHING, INC.

A **DK PUBLISHING BOOK**

Project Editor IRENE LYFORD
Project Art Editor INA STRADINS
DTP Designer MARK BRACEY
Location Photography JAKE FITZJONES
Studio Photography ANDY CRAWFORD, MATTHEW WARD
Stylist SHANI ZION
Production Controller MICHELLE THOMAS
Series Editor CHARLOTTE DAVIES
Series Art Editor CLIVE HAYBALL
US Editor LAAREN BROWN

First American Edition, 1997
2 4 6 8 10 9 7 5 3 1
Published in the United States by DK Publishing, Inc.,
95 Madison Avenue, New York, New York 10016.
Visit us on the World Wide Web at http://www.dk.com

Library of Congress Cataloging in Publication Data
Katz, Sylvia
    One-room living / Sylvia Katz. – 1st American ed.
        p. cm. – (Home design workbooks)
    Includes index.
    ISBN 0-7894-1993-9
    1. Room layout (Dwellings) 2. House furnishings. 3. Apartments.
4. Interior decoration. I. Title. II. Series: DK Home design workbooks.

TX309.K38 1997   97-16626
747'.1–dc21   CIP
Text film output in Great Britain by The Right Type
Reproduced in Singapore by Pica
Printed and bound in Great Britain by Butler & Tanner Ltd
at Frome and London

INTRODUCTION • 6

C O N T E N T S

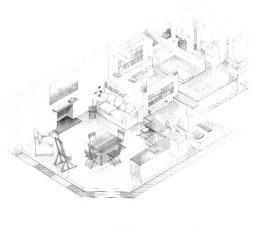

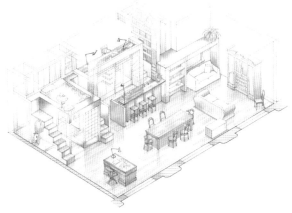

INTRODUCTION

LIVING IN ONE ROOM can be hell. But it can also be fun if you are prepared to be adventurous with space and furniture. Of course "one room" can describe many different shapes and sizes, from a tiny efficiency to a galleried, open-plan apartment. However, the basics remain the same, and it is what you do with them that counts.

For many reasons, both social and cultural, family units are growing smaller, and this, in turn, has created a rising demand for one-room apartments. Couples without children, single professional people, those wanting a city *pied-à-terre*, and separated or divorced people are among the large group of mainly city-dwellers for whom one-room living has become either a choice or a necessity.

Living in one space certainly has economic advantages, such as lower rent, heating, and lighting costs, but it also has enormous creative potential, and it can challenge you to think very clearly about yourself and your lifestyle and to crystallize aspects of your personality and your way of doing things. These will determine the layout of your living space and the furniture and fittings that will make it work for you.

SOURCES OF INSPIRATION

Most of us have experienced life in a confined space, such as a tent, RV, or boat, and have enjoyed it tremendously. What the experience teaches you is the importance of organization, how to reduce your needs to essentials, and how to simplify and streamline your actions. You also learn, through improvisation, how to adapt what you have for other purposes. In the same way, one-room living concentrates the mind and challenges your ingenuity and imagination – there is no room for superfluous baggage.

The inspiration for many of the ideas in this book can be traced to houseboats and barges, Pullman carriages, and cruise ships. Today's motor homes are fitted with sophisticated furnishings that cleverly combine living room, kitchen, dining room, bathroom, and bedroom. When you think about it – and once you have discarded traditional notions of what you actually need in order to live comfortably – you realize that all the necessities for everyday life can be fitted into a few cabinets. A wall of built-in cabinets, containing kitchen, closet, and bed (*see opposite*), has just been incorporated into a London apartment, but many other elegant solutions to one-room living have been inspired by the Japanese approach to life in a minimal,

△ SHIPSHAPE KITCHEN
The galley of a motor yacht illustrates how to pack a complete mini kitchen, with sink, oven, microwave, and burners, into a tiny space.

SLEEPING CAPSULES ▷
The Japanese, familiar with cramped, multifunctional living spaces, devised the capsule hotel as a one-night stop for travelers prepared to put basic amenities above luxury and space.

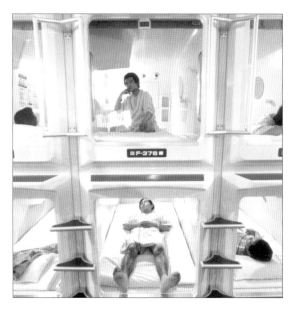

multifunctional space. Sliding, translucent screens provide a flexible way of dividing living areas, while taking up very little space. The futon has been accepted in the West as a simple sofa-bed (although in Japan a futon, without a base, is rolled up and stored during the day.) The capsule hotel may not be to everybody's taste, but it does illustrate how to reduce sleeping accommodation to its most expedient level.

Technological changes in the workplace are another major influence on our living patterns. Innovations such as laptops, modems, and mobile phones, and the introduction of flexible working practices, have liberated us from a fixed workplace, and are blurring the boundaries between home and office, work and leisure.

All of these changes are reflected in a growing market for adaptable, multipurpose, space-saving products, and manufacturers and designers have begun to tailor their designs to satisfy this new demand. Tapering baths, swiveling sinks, and corner options on everything from showers, baths, and sinks to cabinets and storage units are just some of the new product species that are emerging in response to the demands of our new way of living.

In this book we have included some of the best examples of such products and designs to stimulate your search for ways of making the most of a limited living space.

△ **FOLD-AWAY LIVING**
Most of the essentials of one-room living can be fitted into a few cabinets. This wall, finished in Italian-style plaster, hides a fold-out kitchen, a fold-down bed, and a fold-out closet. The doors of the kitchen and the closet contain built-in storage.

INDUSTRIAL SPACE ▽
The conversion of obsolete
industrial buildings has
created a new type of living
space, with exposed beams
and brickwork, and double-
height ceilings that allow for
the construction of a gallery
level and suspended storage.

EVALUATE YOUR ROOM

Examine your room
objectively, picking out
positive features that
can be developed, and
noting the weaker areas
that need improvement.
☐ Are there spaces such
as alcoves and around
chimneys, or understair
areas with the potential
for built-in shelving
and cabinets?
☐ Is there room for a
permanent sleeping
area, or enough ceiling
height to consider
constructing a raised
sleeping platform?
☐ How much sunshine
and natural light does
the room receive during
the day? Which areas of
your room benefit most
from these?
☐ Would it be possible
to enlarge the main
window to full floor-to-
ceiling height, or to
extend it into a balcony
or patio area?
☐ Can more windows
be let into an external
wall if necessary?
☐ Does your room have
access to a garden, roof
terrace, or patio? If not,
are there ledges suitable
for window boxes?

Whether your prospective living space is one
room in a large, converted house, an apartment
with two or three tiny rooms whose dividing
walls can be knocked down to create one large
space, or a spacious loft apartment in a
converted industrial building, your first priority
in planning how to use the space is to look
carefully at your future home. Study its features,
and note the position of all plumbing, electrical,
and gas supplies, the way light enters the
building, and which window offers the best view.
Try to work with the existing structure and
services, not against them, and a plan will begin
to take shape. Basic services can, of course, be
moved if necessary, and remote pumping and
disposal systems are available that allow you to
fit a bathroom or kitchen into a location that
conventional plumbing cannot reach.

Consider your heating options, too, at the
planning stage: radiators, a hot-air system, or
even underfloor heating – a Roman invention
that is currently enjoying a revival. Think, too,
about any structural changes that you might
want to make – such as demolishing walls,

STARTING FROM SCRATCH

If you have the opportunity to start from scratch, your apartment will be specially designed
and unique to you. The "shell and core" method of loft conversion offers plumbed and
wired living spaces ready to be personalized in this way.

❶ A BLANK CANVAS
Plumbing, drainage, and wiring are
installed in the shell. Brickwork has
been cleaned and ceilings plastered.

❷ PLANNING AND BUILDING
Living zones are planned and built
on different levels using a variety of
solid and translucent materials.

❸ A PERSONALIZED SPACE
The final loft space has living and
working areas at varying heights,
each contained and color-defined.

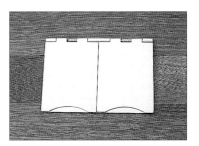

◁ FLOOR SOCKETS
An underfloor power circuit with flush-fitting, floor-mounted sockets provides flexibility in an open space, allowing lights, computers, and audio equipment to be moved around easily.

building a glazed extension, or enlarging or creating windows and doors. For this type of work, you will need to consult an architect who will deal with planning regulations, and help you draw up plans and select materials.

Although overall size will influence what is possible, all one-room living spaces have certain requirements and problems in common. These center on the basic functions of living – cooking, eating, sleeping, washing, working, and relaxing – and these areas and their requirements have been covered in detail in this book. To help focus your ideas, work through our questionnaire *Assess Your Needs* (*see pp.16–17*).

LIVING IN LOFTS

Later in the book, we show examples of different studios and the ingenious ways in which their owners have adapted them to their needs. We

include a number of the loft apartments that are common in some urban areas. Lofts originated in New York in the 1980s, when abandoned warehouses were discovered to have valuable residential potential. The loft movement's mission to salvage disused industrial buildings that might otherwise have been demolished, retaining as much as possible of the original features and industrial dimensions, has been welcomed for helping revitalize run-down inner-city areas.

In this book you will find exciting loft spaces as small as 861 square foot (80 square meters), in which the architects have succeeded in providing the living elements essential for a decent quality of life by employing all the tricks they know for making small spaces appear larger: raised sleeping or work platforms, curved false walls, glass bricks, full-height and full-width mirrors, and frosted glass panels, to name just a few.

Today's designers are also rediscovering age-old furniture forms to suit current lifestyles. Folding, stacking, nesting, hinged, pack-away, and clip-together units can be assembled according to individual needs, and updated versions of old favorites, such as nesting tables, are appearing.

All these devices are invaluable when planning a very limited space. A raised platform releases useful floor space, as well as offering the chance to fill the area below with storage. If you seldom need a dining table, why not store a folded table and a set of trestles out of sight? And, if ceiling height permits, create vital long-term storage space by building a false ceiling to make an "attic," or a raised floor level to form a "cellar."

△ USING BORROWED SPACE
Lateral thinking can solve tricky problems. Here, a washing machine has been fitted into a tiny toilet area by utilizing dead space from the kitchen on the other side of the wall.

△ HOT SPRINGS
Radiators come in all shapes and sizes. This wall-mounted vertical model will fit into a corner or alongside a window.

ABOUT YOU

Before designing your space, you must ask yourself some searching questions: your answers could determine certain choices you have to make *(see p.11.)*

☐ Are you basically an untidy person? Do you have a good storage system, yet have difficulty using it? Are you uncomfortable in a tidy environment?

☐ Are you a workaholic? Do you put your work before leisure, or even before cooking? Do you own a lot of electronic equipment, a library, or a vast amount of files?

☐ Do you entertain often? Is a good deal of your time reserved for cooking, dining, and socializing with friends and family?

☐ Are you a home-maker? Do you prefer to make things yourself rather than buying them in stores?

☐ Do you have hobbies with special equipment that your living space has to accommodate, such as a workbench, or storage space for a surfboard or skiis?

DIVIDING AND DEFINING SPACE

Both physical and visual barriers can be used to separate different areas in a single, open-plan living space: half-height walls, translucent materials, varying floor levels, screens, and movable shelving units – all of these can be employed in imaginative ways.

❶ TRANSLUCENT FABRICS

❷ BAMBOO ROLLER BLINDS

❸ ALUMINUM VENETIAN BLIND

❹ RAISED PLATFORM AREA

❺ VARYING FLOOR FINISHES

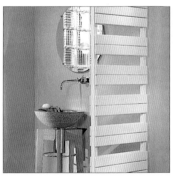
❻ TOWEL RACK/ROOM DIVIDER

❼ DIFFERENT FLOOR LEVELS

❽ HALF-HEIGHT WALLS

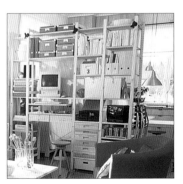
❾ DOUBLE-SIDED SHELVING

◁ PRIVATE SCREENING
A screen can create instant privacy. This one, made of maple veneer panels with translucent, polypropylene hinges, appears to balance with no visible fixings.

One of the fundamental questions you must ask yourself when considering the idea of living in a one-room space is how to deal with the reality of having every aspect of your living arrangements exposed, either within earshot or within view, at all times: having to share the space for living, cooking, working, sleeping, and entertaining. Your solution will depend very much on the type of person you are, so before you start planning your layout you will have to ask yourself some very personal questions and answer them as truthfully as possible if your arrangement is not to backfire on you (*see* "About You," *opposite.*)

Do you need to screen off certain areas for privacy or for peace and quiet, or would you enjoy an open-plan room? Depending on your attitude to these two central questions, you have a choice of dividing up your space in either visual or physical ways. Effective visual barriers can be remarkably simple: a change of flooring from carpet to wood, a switch in floor color, a raised step to another floor level, or simply a large plant in a strategically placed pot. There are also ways of creating visual – but not solid – barriers for privacy, such as draped translucent fabrics, open, double-sided shelving, or vertical towel racks. Equally, there are ways of creating

solid barriers, perhaps for soundproofing reasons, without them being permanent, such as sliding partitions, screens, or cabinets on casters.

Planning and storage are the keys to one-room survival, and this applies particularly to rooms that have to double as home work spaces. Once you have discarded unnecessary furniture and belongings, look for a modular storage system that suits your lifestyle, the nature of your work, and your personality. There has been a tremendous growth in well-designed storage systems, ranging from modular stacking boxes and baskets to industrial fiberboard containers on casters. Many of the high-tech storage containers available have been inspired by the extremely functional products that are to be found in industrial and catering equipment trade catalogs.

For those who like to keep in touch with nature and have difficulty settling for a window-box-sized garden, plants offer another way of dividing one living area from another, as well as adding a hint of nature to an urban setting. A traditional *jardinière* (an ornamental plant stand) can act as a low-level divider, while trailing plants on a high-level shelf soon extend downward to become a natural wall of foliage. Among the new designs available is the plant holder shown (*right*), which consists of a suspended, vertical series of pop-together, transparent plastic bags, each with its own mini water supply. This system can also be used as a decorative fill-in between areas of your living space – but for plants to flourish you must place it close to a good source of natural light.

HANGING GARDEN △
Clear plastic pockets and water sacs provide both an unorthodox indoor garden and an attractive vertical wall decoration, especially if the plants or herbs develop into a cascade of foliage.

We take light for granted, yet it is a valuable tool for changing the shape, color, and dimensions of an interior space. It influences the entire atmosphere of a place and our own feelings as occupants. Take every opportunity to maximize the available natural light and experiment with ways of using it to create a sense of spaciousness.

Light can be reflected around a room through the use of pale-colored paintwork and reflective surfaces such as mirror, glass, laminate, and aluminum slatted blinds. Light can also be transmitted into the darker parts of an interior through clear and frosted glass, glass bricks, translucent paper, fabrics, and blinds. Recessed downlights can create pools of light that act as focal points, and spotlights can be arranged to draw the eye in a certain direction, thereby creating a feeling of space.

MANIPULATING SPACE

An external wall, or a roof that has been exposed by removing a ceiling, provides the possibility of creating another window or a skylight, or an existing window can be enlarged to increase the amount of natural light available. If you have no opportunity to do this, create the illusion of a window by inserting a strip of wall mirror between doors or cupboards. In a similar way, a framed, wall-hung mirror can convey an effective impression of an adjoining room.

You can also manipulate space through the use of different of light fittings, and by the clever use of color. For example, some colors seem to recede while others are more vivid: dark paint will appear to lower a ceiling and bring it nearer,

△ MIRROR IMAGES
Filling a narrow wall space with a strip of mirror is an effective way of creating the illusion of a small window. The mirror will reflect any available light.

while a light, pale color will make it recede.

When confronted with limited space, try to apply the motto of the king of modernism, the architect Mies van der Rohe: "Less is more," and cut back on clutter. But sparseness need not be cold. An overall, light color scheme in a minimalist-style interior creates a feeling of airy space, but the hard edges can be softened with warm wooden floors, carefully selected personal objects, bright acid colors, and plants. Salvaged items and recycled materials, such as reclaimed wood and multicolored plastic sheeting, can be attractive in a home environment, and are particularly valid at a time when we cannot afford to waste materials.

Today there is more need than ever to personalize your own space. Be bold, and reach for what you have always wanted. You are expressing your personality and lifestyle – and, after all, you are the one who must live there.

CREATING LIGHT AND SPACE

Light is particularly important in a small or one-room living space. It can be manipulated to change the feel and shape of a room, through the use of light fixtures, mirror, and glass, and by a careful choice of surface finishes and colors.

❶ ILLUMINATED GLAZED PANEL

❷ GLASS BLOCK WALL

❸ SANDBLASTED GLASS PANEL

❹ "ROOM" IN A MIRROR

❺ MIRROR-DOUBLED SPACE

❻ REFLECTED LIGHT

❼ SHIMMERING METAL BLINDS

❽ WINDOW GARDEN

❾ PATIO KITCHEN EXTENSION

ACTION CHECKLIST

Before you start any alterations or building work, check through the following brief guidelines, which will help you to draw up your plan of action.

☐ Have you made a list of the existing furniture and fixtures that you would like to use in your new living space?

☐ Have you started to collect pictures and samples of designs and products that illustrate what you have in mind?

☐ If you plan to make structural changes, have you been in touch with your local government or spoken to an architect? Even putting up a partition may require a permit.

☐ Have you budgeted carefully for your work plans and materials? Have you thought of setting aside extra for contingencies?

☐ Can you work out a schedule to coordinate the work of builders, plumbers, electricians, and carpenters? Will you be doing any of the work yourself?

HOW THIS BOOK WORKS

THIS BOOK will help you to plan a brand-new apartment or to adapt an existing one by giving you the practical know-how you need to design a home that matches your lifestyle and provides an efficient and comfortable living space. A series of questions helps you assess what you want from your apartment, then a survey of furniture and fixtures guides you to elements that best suit those needs. Three-dimensional plans of six apartments follow, explaining how successful designs have been engineered. Finally, instructions on measuring and drawing up a plan leave you equipped to translate your ideas into reality.

2. SELECT ITEMS ▽

To help you compile a list of the features that will best suit your needs, a range of furniture and fixtures are surveyed (*pp. 18–47.*) A "Remember" box draws your attention to the key design points, and the pros and cons of each element are discussed. Simple diagrams indicate ideal heights for kitchen counters, work equipment, and different kinds of storage, along with advice on moving furniture and work habits.

1. ASSESS YOUR NEEDS ▽

Preliminary questions (*pp. 16–17*) are asked to encourage you to think about your needs and the condition and potential of your present living space. By examining aspects of your lifestyle, such as how you work, relax, and entertain, you will find it easier to identify the most suitable design solutions for remodeling your studio or creating a new one.

4. DESIGNING YOUR APARTMENT △

When you feel satisfied with your ideas, turn to *Plot Your Design* (*pp.74–81*) and put your thoughts into practice. This section provides a step-by-step guide to measuring the whole area, plus detailed instructions on how to draw up a floor plan and wall elevations to scale. Common design mistakes are pinpointed, and successful solutions are shown. Arriving at a satisfactory layout takes time, so draw up variations on tracing paper and select the best elements from each for your final plan.

3. LEARN HOW TO PLAN △

A chapter on *Room Plans* (*pp.48–73*) looks in detail at six existing designs – including loft-style apartments in converted commercial buildings – and offers advice and inspiration on how to bring together all the elements in your own plan. A three-dimensional drawing, a bird's-eye view plan, photographs, and a list of design points explain the thinking behind each design solution, while detailed annotation highlights the most interesting and relevant features.

HOW TO USE THE GRAPH PAPER

■ Draw your room to scale (*see pp.76–81*), using the graph paper provided (*pp.89–96*). You may photocopy if you need more.

■ For a small-scale apartment, use the graph paper with an imperial scale of 1:24, where one large square represents 1ft and one small square represents 3in. Therefore, an area 18in long and 3in wide is drawn as six small squares. Alternatively, use the metric scale of 1:20, where one large square represents 1m and a small square 10cm.

■ For an apartment with larger dimensions, use the graph paper with the smaller scale of 1:48; the large squares represent 4ft and the small squares 6in. Alternatively, use the metric graph paper with the scale of 1:50, where a large square equals 1m and a small square 10cm.

■ Having plotted your room on graph paper, start experimenting with varying designs on overlays of tracing paper.

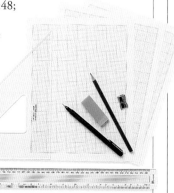

ASSESS YOUR NEEDS

THE FOLLOWING questions will prompt you to consider your lifestyle and needs, area by area, so that as you work through the book you will be able to identify the elements, plans, and style choices that suit you best.

LIVING

The quality and comfort of life in a one-room interior depends on how much space you can create and how well it is adapted to your lifestyle.

☐ Do you find it easiest to relax in a small, intimate area, or do you like the sense of freedom found in a large open space?
☐ Would you prefer to define different areas by varying the floor coverings and wall colors, or do you want to maintain a unified, open-plan space?
☐ Can you arrange your living space to make the most of natural light?
☐ If your space is limited, do you want to keep it uncluttered by using furniture that can be moved aside when it is not needed?
☐ When you have friends visit, are they happy to relax on floor cushions, or would they prefer more conventional seating?
☐ If you have a large collection of books, can they be stored on high-level shelving in spaces that would otherwise be wasted?
☐ Do you have collections of objects that you wish to display? Can they be housed in alcoves or wall cabinets, or would a movable storage unit be more useful?
☐ Would a mini or portable stereo unit be adequate for your needs, or do you have a system that needs special installation?
☐ Would different kinds of lighting for relaxing, reading, or working improve your enjoyment of these activities?
☐ How important is a garden to you? Would a window box or indoor plant display provide a replacement?

COOKING AND EATING

The most important influence on the design of this area is whether you see cooking and eating as important activities or as transient necessities.

☐ Would you like to separate the kitchen in some way, or would you rather include it in the general living space?
☐ When you are working in the kitchen, would you like to face into the living area, or would you prefer an outside view?
☐ Would you like to close off the kitchen, or would you rather make a feature of it by displaying attractive equipment?
☐ Are you a convenience cook, who needs only a microwave oven and a refrigerator, or do you need the space and equipment to prepare adventurous gourmet meals for yourself and guests?
☐ Do you use some pieces of equipment more frequently than others? Can they be stored so that they are accessible, with heavy equipment stored at low levels?
☐ Do you like to sit down at a table for everyday meals, or are you happy with a more informal tray or breakfast bar?
☐ Would you like a dining table that can be extended when necessary, or could you manage with a folding or trestle table that can be put away when not in use?
☐ If space is limited, would a portable or extra-small dishwasher fit? Do you really need such equipment?

☐ If you spend a lot of time in the kitchen area, are you sure that the flooring is durable but "giving" and easy to clean?
☐ Is your cooking area in an unventilated or tight space? Have you considered a hood or garbage disposal unit?

WORKING

The design of your work area depends on whether you are happy working on the kitchen table, or whether you need privacy and a businesslike atmosphere.

☐ If you work at home, do you need a dedicated work space, or would a surface that can be folded away or double as a dining table suffice?
☐ Have you taken into account your realistic day-to-day and long-term work storage needs? Can you plan sufficient file and shelf space near your work area for easy retrieval?
☐ Does your work require specialized equipment? Can you arrange your work space so that there is access to ample outlets and telephone jacks?
☐ Would a specially constructed computer table with shelves for printer and keyboard best suit your needs?
☐ Is good natural light or task lighting essential for your work?
☐ Can you concentrate easily, or do you need some sort of barrier, such as screens or a room divider, to prevent distraction?
☐ Can you adjust your work furniture and equipment in order to achieve maximum comfort and efficiency?
☐ Do you want your work area to look like an office, or would you prefer it to blend in to your interior scheme?
☐ Would screening your work area give a more professional impression when clients visit you?
☐ Is it important to you that your household accounts be well organized and easily accessible?

WASHING

Your bathing habits will determine the layout and design of your bathroom. With imaginative planning, a bath can be installed even in restricted spaces.

☐ Which do you prefer: a shower or a bath? If space is limited, would you consider devoting the entire space to a luxury shower-room, or could you install a space-saving tub?
☐ Do you need a separate bathroom, or could you incorporate a tub or shower stall into your living area?
☐ Can you make use of space above the tub and toilet for bathroom storage? Do you have enough shelves and cabinets for toiletries so that the sink area does not become too cluttered?
☐ If your bathroom is likely to be used by visitors, have you considered how much of the contents you might prefer to conceal?
☐ Do you have the space for a large cabinet for spare towels, or will they have to be stored elsewhere?
☐ Have you made provision for clothes, such as hooks for bathrobes, a laundry hamper, and a bathroom chair?

SLEEPING AND DRESSING

Would you feel happier with a semi-private, defined "bedroom" area, or must the bed double as seating during the daytime, and the sleeping area be used for working and relaxing?

☐ Can you be bothered with the inconvenience of a foldaway bed, or one that doubles as seating during the day, or would you prefer a permanent bed, either on the floor or on a raised platform?
☐ Is privacy in your sleeping area important? Would curtains provide adequate screening, or would you prefer something more substantial?
☐ What do you like to keep by your bed? Have you provided for storage of your alarm clock, reading material, and so on?
☐ If you plan to erect a platform bed, is there a source of natural light and ventilation nearby?
☐ How much hanging, shelf, and drawer space do you need for clothes? How do you like to store out-of-season clothing?
☐ Would you like a dressing area with a full-length mirror and good lighting?
☐ Are you likely to have guests to stay? Do you have room to store a foldaway bed, or could you have seating that doubles as a bed, such as a futon, sofabed, daybed couch, or trundle bed?

UTILITIES

In the early stages of planning, allocate spaces for cleaning-equipment storage and for clothes drying, as well as for the plumbing of a washing machine.

☐ Will you need facilities to do your own laundry, or do you send it out?
☐ If space is limited, would a half-size or stackable washing machine suit you?
☐ Will you need to install a clothes-drying rack or pulley, or do you have a drier?

☐ Have you planned for a ventilated cupboard for storing cleaning products and bulky cleaning equipment?
☐ Could you have a space-saving fold-out ironing table fitted into a kitchen unit, or do you have room for a full-size model?

STORAGE

A good storage system is an absolute necessity for one-room living in order to reduce clutter and keep belongings in some degree of order.

☐ Do you prefer to hide clutter behind doors, or do you like the idea of using open containers, such as baskets and hanging wall pockets?
☐ Will you need space for long-term storage, such as gardening and sports equipment, tools, and craft supplies?
☐ If you don't want a built-in appearance in your kitchen, can you adapt existing pieces of furniture for storage?
☐ Do you have equipment that requires storage at a controlled temperature?
☐ Will items in long-term storage need protection from dust and insects?
☐ If you have valuables, is it worth investing in a safe for security?

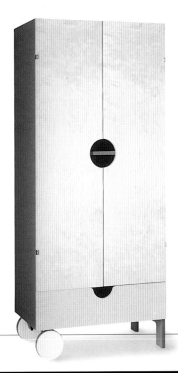

LIVING AREA

WHEN SPACE IS LIMITED, multifunctional furniture is the most practical choice. Look for sofas that convert to beds and for folding and stacking chairs that can be hung on the wall or stored in a corner when not in use. Nesting tables are intrinsically space-saving, while portable pieces are extremely versatile. Make use of any spaces inside and under seating by packing them with storage containers.

FLEXIBLE SEATING

Two types of seating are particularly well suited to one-room living: modular pieces provide maximum flexibility and function, as well as comfort, whereas minimal seating, which can be folded up or stacked when not in use, is ideal for maximizing the use of limited space.

INTERLOCKING PIECES
The sections of this fabric-covered foam seating system also fit together to form a block that can be laid horizontally, to provide an occasional double bed, or arranged vertically, to form a sculpted screen.

SIMPLE CONSTRUCTION
Polyurethane foam is cut to shape and covered in stretch jersey fabric.

CONVERSATION PIECE
Modular seating allows the flexibility of arranging the pieces to meet the demands of any social occasion.

FOLDING CHAIR △
An up-to-date version of an old favorite, this brushed aluminum chair with canvas seat and back is comfortable, lightweight, and easily stored when not in use.

MODULAR SEATING △
Designed originally in the 1960s, these fabric-covered foam shapes are practical and fun. In addition to offering endless seating permutations to suit a variety of lifestyles and interiors, they can double as a spare bed (*see above*).

CONVERTIBLE SEATING ▷
Sofas that convert to beds are available in many shapes and sizes, including the traditional folding version with integral mattress, and futons on folding bases. Shown here is a studio couch that opens sideways to become a single bed.

ADAPTABLE TABLES

While there is always a need for small side tables, in restricted living spaces the emphasis must be on versatile units that not only provide convenient surfaces but also double as stools or storage units. Look for designs that offer extra flexibility, such as folding, nesting, and extending tables, or units on casters that can be moved easily from one part of the apartment to another as they are required.

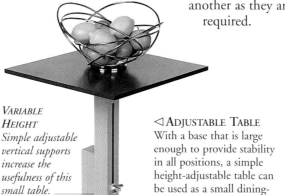

VARIABLE HEIGHT
Simple adjustable vertical supports increase the usefulness of this small table.

◁ **ADJUSTABLE TABLE**
With a base that is large enough to provide stability in all positions, a simple height-adjustable table can be used as a small dining-table or plant stand.

△ **SPACE-SAVING SEATING**
When not in use this ingenious version of the trundle bed slides under the low-level platform unit – which serves as a seating area – leaving the spaciousness of the interior undiminished.

REMEMBER

■ Choose modular furniture that allows you to arrange the pieces to suit your particular requirements.

■ Look for mechanisms and fittings that transform single items into multifunctional pieces of furniture.

■ Hide clutter in storage boxes and drawers that fit into all available space in and around furniture.

■ Choose furniture that is well designed and well made: cheaper products can be a false economy unless intended for a limited life.

■ Maximize the use of walls for storage by hanging up furniture and other items.

△ **NESTING TABLES AND CHEST**
Space-saving nesting tables are widely available. This imaginative Italian design has extended the idea to include a small chest of drawers.

VERSATILITY
Both the top and the base fold flat for hanging on the wall.

WALL-HUNG TABLE/PICTURE ▷
This unusual design, made in beech, steel, and glass, offers more than a side table: a picture or photograph of your choice can be displayed beneath the clipped-on glass top. When the table is folded up it can be displayed on the wall as a work of art.

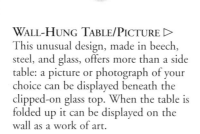

△ **OPEN TABLE**   △ **FOLDED TABLE**

BEECH FRAMEWORK
The main structure of the unit is made from polished beech-veneered plywood.

ALUMINUM ADDITIONS
Sheet aluminum has been cut and folded to form the drawers and legs.

▽ **TABLE-CHEST**
Look for multipurpose designs, such as this beautifully made, beech-veneered table-chest. The clever use of hinges allows for easy adaptation from space-saving chest of drawers to low table, without disturbing the contents of the two aluminum drawers.

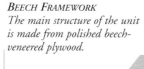

TABLE WITH STORAGE
Innovative design allows the unit to be easily adapted from chest to table.

STORAGE AND DISPLAY

Flexible storage is vital for maintaining a sense of uncluttered space in a studio or loft. Fixed, free-standing cabinets take up space, but mobile pieces can be moved around to suit different occasions. Think laterally and discover unexpected places for positioning shelves and cabinets, such as the doorway between one room and another, where a false passage filled with shelving can be created. Glass shelving provides an attractive method of displaying favorite objects and collections, without interrupting the surrounding flow of light and space.

CORRECT LIFTING

Keep your back straight and bend your knees to avoid back injury.

When lifting heavy objects keep your back straight and bend your knees, then slowly straighten into the upright position.

REMEMBER

■ Assess every corner space for its storage potential. Even very narrow gaps can be fitted with small shelves for CDs, or used to store sports equipment.

■ Add casters to furniture so that you can easily alter the interior layout. Bookshelves can be moved to provide an instant screen, while storage chests can double as tables.

■ Make the most of walls and ceilings for storage purposes, thus freeing limited floor space.

▽ COLORFUL CUBE
Based on the idea of a refrigerator-door, the interlocking door of this cabinet forms part of the storage space. The unit is mounted on five casters, one of which is on the door.

MOBILE STORAGE
Providing an attractive display cabinet when open, this mobile unit doubles as a side table.

△ NO WASTED SPACE
With a variety of cabinets and shelves, this wall is entirely filled with storage, while the doorway to the adjoining room has been converted into a passage with shelving. White paintwork gives a light and spacious feeling to this intensively used space.

DOUBLE-SIDED STORAGE
With sections large enough to hold a mini sound system or stacks of boxes, this unit is a versatile piece of furniture.

STORAGE DIVIDER ▷
Measuring 68in (173cm) high by 64in (163cm) wide, this beech-veneered storage unit on locking steel wheels can act as both a temporary room divider and as a multipurpose storage unit with access from both sides.

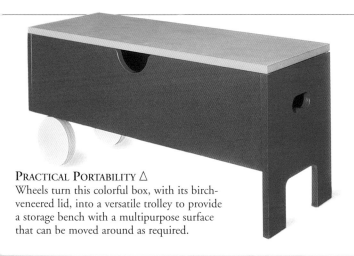

PRACTICAL PORTABILITY △
Wheels turn this colorful box, with its birch-veneered lid, into a versatile trolley to provide a storage bench with a multipurpose surface that can be moved around as required.

AUDIOVISUAL ENTERTAINMENT

In a small space, the storage of audiovisual equipment calls for ingenious solutions. Wall brackets, designed for televisions and speakers, free valuable floor space, while mobile television and video carts allow equipment to be wheeled out of sight when not in use.

△ STORAGE AS SCULPTURE
Among the wide and imaginative range of CD racks now available, from freestanding towers to slot-together systems, this simple and elegant model in natural wood turns CD storage into a wall-mounted work of art.

ALL-AROUND VIEWING △
This well-made, wall-mounted steel and alloy television support has a tilt and swivel action that allows the set to be viewed from any position in the apartment.

SWIVELING SHELF
The swiveling top section increases the versatility of this television and video cart.

DOUBLE-SIDED
Accessible from both sides, the shelf spaces of this unit can be used for CD or video storage.

△ MOBILE TELEVISION CART
Mobile pieces of furniture, such as this solid beech storage unit, are particularly useful in restricted living spaces, where it is often convenient to move items out of the way when they are not being used. This unit, although designed for television or sound-system storage, could equally well be used for work storage or as a handy bedside cabinet. The unit is mounted on rubber-tired casters for easy movement.

COOKING AREA

RECREATIONAL VEHICLES AND BOATS provide good examples of the organization and streamlined, logical planning that are the key to successful cooking in a small space. The first step is to take account of how you shop and cook, so that you can make informed decisions about what equipment you need.

STOVES AND FRESH-FOOD STORAGE

Limit yourself to two burners – unless you honestly think that you need more – and opt instead for cooking methods that are both space- and energy-saving, such as multitiered pans, slow cookers, and microwave ovens. However little cooking you do, you will need storage for perishable food. Refrigerators come in all sizes and styles, including tabletop and slimline models.

HEAVY DOORS
Each of the extra-wide doors is hung on four hinges and reinforced down the hinge side.

KITCHEN SINK
Neatly incorporated into the unit are a small sink, drainer, and two hot plates.

HIDDEN KITCHEN
Two doors, each lined with shelves from top to bottom, open to reveal a self-contained, fully fitted kitchen.

△ TRIPLE SAUCEPAN SET
Cook a whole meal on one burner in this classic three-part saucepan – an economy that is as relevant today as when the set was first designed.

△ MULTITIERED COOKING
Based on the Indian and Chinese method of stacking containers over one heat source, this is a supremely efficient cooking system.

COMPLETE KITCHEN ▷
As a ready-assembled unit, this self-contained mini kitchen is ready to be fitted and connected to power sources and plumbing. It provides a neat solution to food preparation in a very restricted space.

BUILT-IN MICROWAVE OVEN
The inclusion of a microwave oven is a boon to those with busy lifestyles and extends the range of cooking options.

FULL-SIZE REFRIGERATOR
Although the whole unit measures only 39 x 23 x 35in (1000 x 600 x 900mm), refrigerator capacity is not reduced.

WALL OF DOORS
The external doors of the kitchen, and of the other cabinets along this wall, have a special marmorino plaster finish, made with lime and marble dust.

△ **KITCHEN IN A CUPBOARD**
The generous dimensions of this elegant cupboard kitchen provide ample storage space for china and nonperishable supplies on the shelves that line the inner surface of the doors. Downward-flowing light from a narrow glazed roof light illuminates the kitchen counter.

MOBILE WORK SURFACE ▷
A mobile food preparation surface, such as this maplewood cart, is very useful in small spaces. This model, at standard counter height, has a deep drawer, a hanging rail for utensils, and a pull-out shelf.

WORKTOP HEIGHT

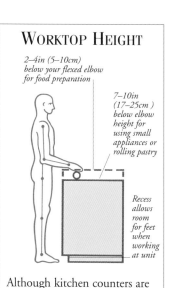

2–4in (5–10cm) below your flexed elbow for food preparation

7–10in (17–25cm) below elbow height for using small appliances or rolling pastry

Recess allows room for feet when working at unit

Although kitchen counters are a standard height, it is useful to have a lower surface for certain food preparation processes.

REMEMBER

■ Make a realistic assessment of your cooking requirements and plan accordingly. If you live alone or cook very little, you may not need a traditional-style kitchen.

■ If you do not have room for even a tabletop refrigerator, consider storing fruit and vegetables in a pantry or outside storeroom where they will keep fresh longer.

■ Combination ovens provide the speed and compact design of a microwave oven along with the advantages of a convection oven and broiler.

■ Make sure that there is a heat-resistant surface next to the stove so that hot pots and pans will not cause damage.

■ Consider your shopping and cooking habits when buying a refrigerator, and choose a suitable model.

COUNTERTOP APPLIANCES

An increasing choice of scaled-down, tabletop versions of standard kitchen appliances, including stoves, is now available. To this can be added a range of countertop cooking appliances: toaster ovens, electric grills and griddles, electric woks, and even an electric oven that bakes, roasts, and grills.

△ **CLASSIC COMPACT STOVE**
Designed to sit on a kitchen counter, or on the optional fold-flat stand, this updated version of a classic compact stove includes two hotplates, an oven, and a broiler.

△ **ELECTRIC SKILLET**
Electric skillets, available in many sizes, present great possibilities for imaginative and economical one-pan cooking, and many are attractive enough to be brought to the table for serving.

△ **DORMITORY REFRIGERATOR**
If space is tight, look for a mini refrigerator like this model, which features a small freezer and room for several bottles in the door, but is small enough to fit on a kitchen counter.

KITCHEN STORAGE SYSTEMS

When space is limited, it is vital that none of it is wasted or overlooked. The simple units designed originally for warehouse and factory use are especially space-saving, and have been successfully assimilated into domestic interiors. Make full use of wall and ceiling space: a ceiling rail with hooks provides convenient storage for saucepans and other cooking utensils.

WALL-HANGING SYSTEMS ▷
Clear clutter off the work surface and create more working space by hanging utensils on the walls. A wall-mounted rail and hook system offers flexibility by allowing pots and pans and cooking implements to be stored in the most convenient location.

SAUCEPAN STAND
Make the most of a corner space with this multitiered saucepan stand.

HANGING UTENSILS
Essential cooking utensils hang on the wall above the stove.

◁ VERTICAL SPACE
Vertical systems can provide a useful amount of kitchen storage while occupying minimal floor space. Consider narrow shelves or suspended tiers of wire vegetable baskets.

DRAWER STORAGE
Infrequently used kitchen equipment is stored in drawer units next to and underneath the built-in oven.

△ AWKWARD CORNER
A corner space becomes easily accessible with pull-out cantilevered trays. Use the space to store bulky saucepans and infrequently used kitchen equipment.

PULL-OUT PANTRY ▷
Pull-out storage units with adjustable shelves maximize deep wall space. Designed to carry heavy loads, they hold a surprising number of packets and cans.

FLEXIBLE WALL SYSTEM ▷
Modular wall storage systems, such as the one shown here, provide the opportunity to select and arrange components according to individual taste and requirements, as well as being a convenient, easily accessible method of storage.

Spice jars, oil and vinegar bottles, spoon baskets, fresh herbs in pots, paper towel holders, and bunches of garlic can all be displayed, along with purely decorative items.

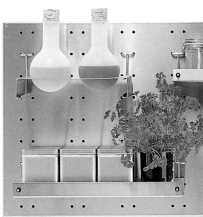

DISHWASHING AND WASTE DISPOSAL

Manufacturers have responded to the needs of people living on their own in small spaces by producing countertop mini dishwashers and ultra-slim models that fit underneath counters, as well as ingenious space-saving sinks. Waste disposal units are ideal for high-rise dwellers, but they require correctly sized waste pipes and a second sink to work effectively.

◁ **DISHWASHER**
Dealing immediately with dirty dishes and pans helps keep a small living space tidy. Dishwashers designed to sit on a kitchen counter, yet offering a normal range of washing and drying options, provide one solution to the problem.

△ **SLIMLINE DISHWASHER**
This compact dishwasher is ideal for one-room living and can be slotted into a gap beneath a kitchen counter, provided the water supply and water pipes are within reach.

ADAPTABLE KITCHEN SINK ▽
Look for sinks that offer a choice of accessories such as extra work surfaces and draining baskets. To satisfy the growing consumer demand for colors, traditional stainless steel sinks are now being challenged by sculptural designs in composite resin that feels like ceramic.

DISH RACK
An efficient metal drainer fits over the sink instead of taking up counter space.

VERSATILE DRAINER
This two-sectioned plastic drainer is a practical and space-saving device.

SPICE SHELF
Jars of colorful spices provide an attractive and useful display.

WALL PANEL
Specially designed for small spaces, this system consists of a stainless steel wall panel and a range of hooks, bars, and shelves.

◁ **WASTE DISPOSAL**
An alternative to the free-standing garbage can or door-hung, swing-out can, this simple method for disposing of organic waste can be adapted to fit under existing counters.

RECYCLING WASTE ▷
With the growing trend for separating and recycling kitchen waste – and for avid gardeners who choose to make their own compost – separate bins for organic and inorganic matter are a sensible option.

DINING AREA

THE EXTENT OF YOUR ENJOYMENT of food and cooking, and your preference for eating quickly or dining at leisure, must exert a strong influence on your choice of furniture and accessories for this area. But, with planning and imagination, the difficulties of eating and entertaining in a tight space can be resolved, so that dirty dishes are quickly cleared from view, and extra tables and chairs can be folded away or stacked in a corner when not in use.

VERSATILE BREAKFAST BARS

If you prefer a simple, informal eating area for everyday use, breakfast bars provide a neat and space-efficient option. Choose from a traditional, fixed peninsular bar, a kitchen counter with diner-style high stools – which may partially separate the cooking and living areas – or a hinged, wall-hung table that can be fitted into any suitable wall space and supported by a leg or a bracket that folds flat after use. If possible, site your breakfast bar where you can enjoy the morning sun.

△ PULL-OUT BREAKFAST BAR
Concealed behind a false drawer front, this pull-out breakfast bar with drop-down leg supports is an ingenious extension of the counter. It can be quickly set up, and concealed when not in use, yet takes up only the space of one drawer in a standard kitchen unit.

◁ **CORNER TABLE FOR TWO**
When living in a restricted space, do not overlook any space, however small or awkwardly shaped: small tables can be designed to fit into the most surprising places. This example, supported on one leg, is built into a small, unused corner space.

▽ **HIGH-TECH SOLUTION**
An elegant method of concealing the cooking area in a studio or loft is to install a blind. In this high-tech loft, the kitchen area is screened off by a remote-controlled aluminum venetian blind. A dramatic lighting effect is created by switching on the kitchen counter can lights when the blind is lowered.

FOLDING AND STACKING TABLES AND CHAIRS

Furniture that can be packed away saves a lot of space and reduces clutter, while a block of colorful stacking chairs can form an attractive interior feature. Folding chairs can be propped against the wall or hung decoratively on hooks or Shaker peg racks, liberating valuable floor space. Echoes of camping equipment are evident in these designs, which are based on adaptability and the use of strong, lightweight materials.

STACKING CHAIRS
Several of these chairs can be stored in a small area.

SUPPLEMENTARY SEATING △
Stacking chairs are a neat solution to additional seating requirements for those living in small spaces.

EASY STORAGE
A folding table can be propped against the wall or stored in a closet when not in use, while stacking chairs take up little space.

◁ **LIGHTWEIGHT FURNITURE**
A lightweight aluminum folding table and stacking chairs, which complement the aluminum blinds running the length of this minimalist loft, can be easily hidden away after use, leaving the uncluttered spaciousness of the apartment to be appreciated.

REMEMBER

■ Choose a kitchen bar for convenient everyday eating, bringing out a folding or trestle table for more formal dining.

■ Try to position the dining area in the sunniest part of the room to benefit from the morning or afternoon light.

■ Analyze your cooking and eating patterns carefully, then select furniture accordingly.

■ Look for imaginative ways to screen off the cooking area and to store tables and chairs when they are not in use.

OUTDOOR-INDOOR EATING ▷
Garden-style folding furniture, bathed in light streaming through the full-width window, creates a sense of the outdoor patio area extending into the interior.

WORK AREA

THE KEY TO WORKING FROM HOME when space is limited or shared is an efficient filing system that allows the work area to be kept as tidy and contained as possible. A home office can be built from a combination of fixed and mobile units, or you may choose a hinged, fold-away desk, a simple worktop on trestles, or even a traditional bureau with a drop-down surface.

FLEXIBLE WORKSTATIONS

A work unit that can be easily moved out of sight or folded away when not in use makes an idea home office in a restricted living space. Look for a design that will provide ample storage space for all your work-related equipment, files, and accessories, as well as features such as pull-out sections and adjustable shelving for maximum flexibility.

HINGED DESK ▷
Two hinged surfaces – one providing the work area, the other providing its support – fold flat against the wall when not in use. This imaginative idea, although simple and inexpensive, provides a generous amount of work space when required, yet takes up very little room when folded away.

MONITOR POSITION
To prevent eyestrain, adjust the position of the monitor to suit your height and line of vision.

PIVOTING BASE
An adjustable base allows the position of the monitor to be easily changed.

SWIVEL SUPPORT
Further flexibility in positioning the monitor is provided by the swiveling steel support.

COMPUTER STORAGE
A hard drive is stored vertically in one of the internal door sections.

HOME OFFICE ▷
Constructed from MDF (medium-density fiberboard) and translucent plastic on a steel frame, this ingenious home office provides storage for computer equipment and files in the door section, and a pivoting, adjustable shelf to hold a computer monitor. The whole unit can be closed up when not in use.

OUT OF SIGHT
The unit, on casters for easy mobility, closes to form a neat "cube."

PULL-OUT PRINTER SHELF
The sliding shelf, holding a printer or other peripheral device, can be pushed back when not in use.

◁ CONCEALED DESK
When the hinged work surface and its support are folded away, the desk is concealed, leaving an uncluttered space in front of the kitchen work area.

FOLD-AWAY SURFACE
The work surface folds flat against the back of the kitchen unit.

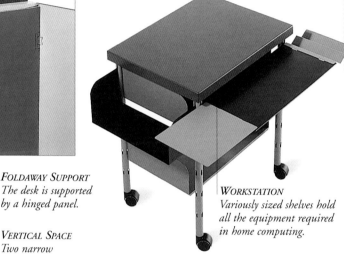

FOLDAWAY SUPPORT
The desk is supported by a hinged panel.

VERTICAL SPACE
Two narrow shelves, one above the other, provide storage space for a surprising number of vertical files.

WORKSTATION
Variously sized shelves hold all the equipment required in home computing.

SPACE-SAVING COMPUTER CART △
Computer carts, designed to hold computer, monitor, keyboard, printer, and other equipment, are widely available and, like this lightweight, painted steel model, have the advantage of being easily moved out of sight when not in use. They can also be used to hold a television set or stereo system.

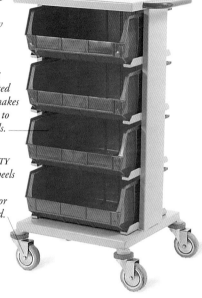

FILING SYSTEMS
A wide choice of filing and work storage systems is available, including wall-hung, stacking, and mobile units. Vertically arranged designs offer the maximum storage capacity while occupying the least amount of floor space; multifunctional mobile units are also useful in tight spaces.

WALL UNIT
Make good use of odd spaces with a narrow wall unit.

AT A GLANCE
An open-fronted storage unit makes for easy access to work and tools.

EASY MOBILITY
Storage on wheels can be easily pushed away or turned around.

△ VERTICAL POCKETS
Made of galvanized metal, this slim, vertical pocket system will fit into the narrowest gap, yet provides useful space for storage or display. A horizontal version is equally effective.

△ MOBILE STORAGE SYSTEM
Industrial storage systems often include well-designed, robustly constructed units that are ideal for the home office. This useful storage cart, with open-fronted drawers, can be easily moved around.

SPLASH OF COLOR
Painted and lacquered MDF (medium-density fiberboard), provides the color in this functional design.

STEADY WORK
Casters with brakes prevent the unit from moving while work is in progress.

WORKING POSITION

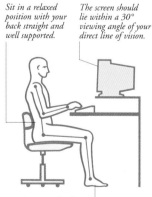

Sit in a relaxed position with your back straight and well supported.

The screen should lie within a 30° viewing angle of your direct line of vision.

Keep your feet flat on the floor; use a foot rest if the chair is too high.

When work involves sitting at a desk for long periods, good posture and correct positioning of equipment are vital.

FIBERBOARD BOXES △
These durable black fiberboard boxes are available in a variety of sizes and designs, and form part of a range of containers that can be used individually or stacked.

REMEMBER

■ Look for flexible, space-saving systems, such as modular stacking boxes, wall-mounted plastic tray systems, and stacking units on wheels.

■ Give a a secondhand metal filing cabinet a new lease on life by respraying it in a color to match your decor.

■ Don't put design and style before personal comfort. Make sure that monitor, desk, chair, and keyboard heights are all correctly adjusted.

■ Enhance your living space by hiding unattractive office equipment behind cabinet doors or screens.

WASHING AREA

WHEN PLANNING YOUR BATHROOM, think beyond the limitations of the existing hot and cold water supply and waste stack positions: pipework can always be moved, thereby providing many new possibilities for the location and size of your washing area. Choose from a wide variety of space-efficient designs – from corner baths and showers to modern sitz baths.

BATHS AND SHOWERS

Showers are convenient, economical, fast, and ideal in restricted spaces. For those who prefer a relaxing bath, however, a range of ingenious designs allows a tub to be fitted into the most awkward area. Some baths are wider at one end than the other, while others fit neatly across a corner.

SHOWER-ROOM ▷
Although there is enough space to fit a bath in this high-tech shower room, with its salvaged steel basin and exposed pipework, the entire width has been fitted instead with a custom-made steel shower tray, with an extra-large shower rose. A frosted glass panel allows natural light to enter the area.

REMEMBER

■ When choosing a shower, check that the unit suits the water pressure and flow rate of your plumbing system.

■ Discuss your bathroom plans with a qualified plumber and electrician before starting work.

■ Standards for plumbing components vary from country to country, so be sure to select the appropriate system.

■ Remember to leave adequate space for movement around each piece of equipment.

■ A ventilation fan must be fitted in an internal bathroom or shower-room to prevent damp and condensation.

■ Hide the unsightly clutter of pipework and cisterns behind fitted cabinets and semi-recessed vanity units.

■ Enjoy the free luxury of washing in sunlight by clever positioning of a shower or bath.

■ When planning a bathroom, consider the benefit of fitting a heated towel rail.

CREATIVE SOLUTION ▷
This sunken bath is a unique space-saving feature: with the bed rolled back and the blinds down, a private bathing area is created, with interesting light effects produced by the underwater lighting. There is generous storage space beneath the decking constructed from reclaimed Scottish pitch pine.

CORNER SHOWER UNIT △
Showers are ideal when space is limited, since they can be fit into any corner or be incorporated into wardrobe units. Shower panels must be made of toughened safety glass.

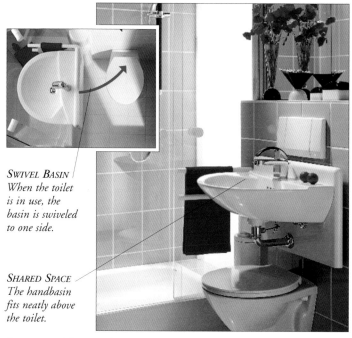

CLEVER BASINS

Washbasins come in an exciting variety of shapes, sizes, and materials, but in small bathrooms, where space is at a premium, it is crucial that you select a model that is large enough for your needs yet avoids wasting space. For example, a basin can be wall-hung on brackets or semi-recessed into a cabinet unit, both options allowing for storage space below.

SWIVEL BASIN
When the toilet is in use, the basin is swiveled to one side.

SHARED SPACE
The handbasin fits neatly above the toilet.

ADAPTABLE DESIGN △
The preplumbed panel of this clever space-saving unit with swiveling handbasin contains hot and cold water and waste pipes, and allows for an individual choice of basin and toilet to be installed.

REMOVABLE LEGS
The legs can be removed and the tub fitted into a built-in unit.

SPACE-SAVING BATH △
Providing a compromise between a shower and a bath when space is limited, the sitz bath is an option for those who prefer bathing in comfort. Traditional in design, it takes up little space and is ideal for a small bathroom, bedroom, or even under the stairs.

UNDERBED STORAGE
Deep storage drawers are built into the space beneath the double bed.

SMOOTH MOVEMENT
The rubber rollers of the bed run in channels, making it easy to move despite its weight.

BATH SHELF
A generous shelf space for storing toiletries has been built around the bath, like the deck of a boat.

BATH LIGHT
The bath water, lit up by an underwater light installed in the base, throws reflections onto the ceiling.

BRIGHT CORNER
White paint and a sunny position ensure that this corner is bright with reflected light.

EXTRA STORAGE
Additional storage space has been created under the vanity basin in the remodeled wall.

△ CREATIVE WALLS
This wall looks like an original feature, but it has been newly constructed, with a small vanity basin, glass shelf, and cupboard built into an alcove where they are almost invisible from the rest of the studio apartment.

SLEEPING AREA

MANY OF THE IDEAS for fitting beds into small spaces, such as the trundle bed or the Japanese futon, are based on traditional designs. Other space-saving solutions, such as foldaway beds and raised beds with storage drawers below, originate from cabin and RV fittings. A major question is whether the bed has to double as seating during the day, or whether it can be concealed when not in use.

SIMPLE STORAGE
On the reverse side to the bed is a storage unit for TV and audio equipment.

FOLDDOWN BEDS

The main advantage of a bed that folds up into the wall during the daytime is that it frees a considerable amount of living space. The bed is concealed behind a vertical surface that can be used for decorative purposes. The disadvantage is that bedding must be packed away when the bed is not in use, which may prove inconvenient when done on a daily basis.

ADAPTABLE SCREEN/BED ▷
A good example of an adaptable, multipurpose design, this screen/bed has shelving for audio equipment, CDs, and magazines on one side and, on the other, a hydraulically operated, pulldown bed. Pivoting side units on either side of the bed open out to create a contained sleeping area behind the screen, which is finished on both sides with a decorative paneled effect.

HANGING SPACE
Hooks set into the angled roof space create a small front-facing closet.

DOOR SHELVING
The interior surface of the wardrobe door is fitted with useful storage shelves.

PAINTED MDF
The main structure of the unit is made from medium-density fiberboard (MDF.)

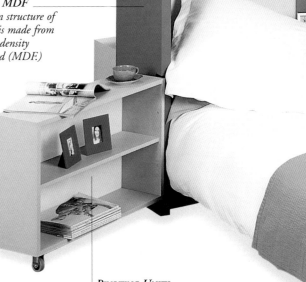

EASY OPENING
A hydraulic system enables the bed panel to be opened and closed with ease.

CONCEALED BED AND CLOSET △
The pull-down bed and the closet next to it are both completely concealed behind large panels. These have been treated with a special Italian-style tinted plaster finish to provide a neutral backdrop for furniture. The bed alcove, which includes a shelf for books and alarm clock, is illuminated by halogen spotlights.

PIVOTING UNITS
The side units pivot outward, supported on casters, to provide useful bedside storage.

BED CLOSED
*The bed is folded up
and the side units closed.*

REMEMBER

■ A good bed is a necessity. If you are buying a new one, test it thoroughly to make sure that it is right for you.

■ A wall bed for guests can be installed wherever there is floor space, no matter how unlikely the position. Create instant privacy with a screen.

■ When constructing a raised bed platform, check all safety aspects, including the rails and ladder. Check also that there is enough headroom between the platform and the ceiling.

■ Bedding can be stored in a wooden blanket chest, which doubles as a side table, or in underbed storage containers.

■ Unless you have an antique bed that you wish to feature in your sleeping area, consider a furniture system that allows you to adapt the shape and layout as your life changes.

DUAL-PURPOSE BEDS

A bed is one of the most important and one of the largest items in any living space. So, when space is limited, it is vital to choose one that earns its keep by doubling as seating or storage – or both – during the day, as well as providing a comfortable place to sleep at night.

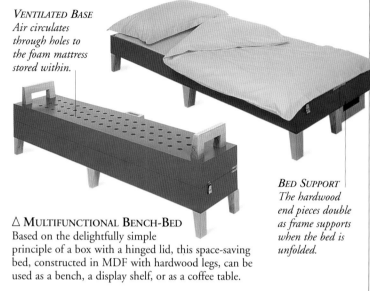

VENTILATED BASE
Air circulates through holes to the foam mattress stored within.

BED SUPPORT
The hardwood end pieces double as frame supports when the bed is unfolded.

△ **MULTIFUNCTIONAL BENCH-BED**
Based on the delightfully simple principle of a box with a hinged lid, this space-saving bed, constructed in MDF with hardwood legs, can be used as a bench, a display shelf, or as a coffee table.

PANELED EFFECT
A decorative effect is achieved by covering the vertical panels with squares of ³⁄₁₆in (5mm) MDF.

TRANSLUCENT BACK
The side units and a small alcove above the bed are backed with translucent plastic.

△ **ROOM WITHIN A ROOM**
The construction of this softwood platform bed has created generous study space below, with room for shelving and storage units.

▽ **UNDERBED STORAGE**
The space beneath a bed is ideal for storage – whether in deep drawers, movable containers, or zipped bags – or, as here, for a spare bed.

HINGED BASEBOARD
When the bed is folded up, this baseboard hangs flat.

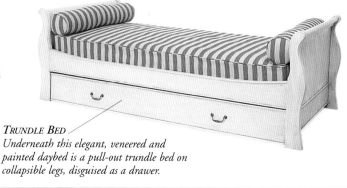

TRUNDLE BED
Underneath this elegant, veneered and painted daybed is a pull-out trundle bed on collapsible legs, disguised as a drawer.

UTILITY AREA

CLEVER MECHANISMS AND FITTINGS provide the key to storing basic appliances and cleaning equipment so that they are easily accessible and do not create unsightly clutter in a restricted living space. Indeed, the quality of life in one-room living depends very much on such hidden services. Concealed or not, however, stored objects are usable only if they are tidily organized in a practical, modular storage system.

STORING EQUIPMENT

Solutions to storing cleaning equipment range from simple, imaginative ideas to integrated appliances. Industrial systems such as pull-out pantries, formerly found only in warehouses and factories, are now being appropriated by the domestic market because they are so practical and use a minimum of materials.

WIRE RACK STORAGE SYSTEMS ▷
In restricted areas, wire rack and basket systems provide an invaluable and flexible method of storage. They can be fit into virtually any space, whether under the stairs or on the backs of cupboard doors. They do not gather dust and everything that is stored is immediately visible and accessible. Hooks and small containers can be added to extend their storage possibilities.

NO CLUTTER
Use wall brackets and clips to hold vacuum cleaners, extension tubes, and tools neatly in place.

SPACE SAVERS
Wire racks, of stainless steel or plastic-coated wire, are widely available in a range of designs.

LARGE ITEMS
Ensure that there is room for large items such as a vacuum cleaner, ironing board, and buckets.

REMEMBER

■ Reduce clutter by fitting racks and baskets, hooks, and hanging pockets on the backs of cabinet doors and inside any useful concealed space

■ Make the best use of hard-to-reach corner spaces under counters by installing carousel storage trays.

■ Store dusters and shoe-cleaning equipment in bags hung inside cabinets.

■ Good ventilation is vital for areas where cleaning products and equipment are stored.

■ Marine-grade plywood is impervious to moisture and steam, and is an ideal material to use in poorly ventilated kitchens and washing areas.

◁ **SIMPLE SOLUTIONS**
One cheap and cheerful solution to storage is a simple fabric "shoebag" that can be hung up wherever there is space. Other inexpensive ideas include colorful plastic baskets and stacking boxes and crates.

▽ UNDERSTAIRS UTILITY ROOM

Despite its location under the stairs, this utility room – which houses a washer-dryer as well as other essential household equipment – appears spacious. The bright color scheme and the full-width mirror in the adjacent washing area not only help create an airy feeling, but also seem to double the size of this internal room.

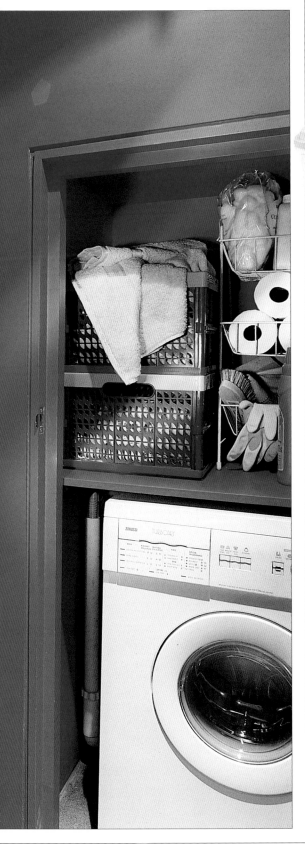

LAUNDRY FACILITIES

The requirements of people living alone or in small spaces has resulted in a new generation of compact washing and drying machines. When teamed with retractable ironing boards and high-level clothes-drying racks, these basic services take up very little space and may even be concealed entirely from view.

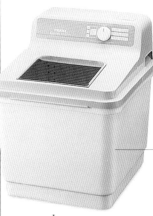

◁ MINI WASHER
Compact clothes-washing machines, which are designed to sit on a sink drainer and to be put away when not in use, are ideal for those living in restricted spaces.

SINK-TOP WASHING Easily connected to a hot water supply, this top-loading machine is simple to use.

△ SLIMLINE MODEL
Perfect for a small utility cupboard or narrow space, a slimline washing machine takes up much less room than a standard front-loading model.

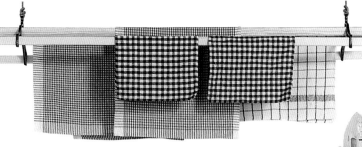

TRADITIONAL PULLEY △
A simple rise-and-fall "pulley," made of plastic-coated steel or natural wood, provides one of the most space-saving methods of drying and airing laundry.

HANGING BRACKETS ▷
When space is restricted, hang appliances on the wall rather than prop them up. Look in industrial catalogs for the most suitable brackets.

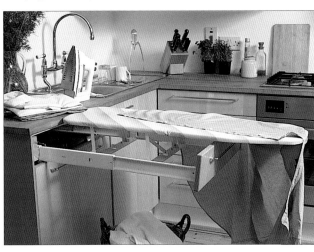

△ FOLD-AWAY IRONING BOARD
Stored behind a false drawer front in a sink unit, this pull-out, folding ironing board includes an extra extension for ironing sleeves. The telescopic supporting brackets are part of an extensive range of mechanisms designed to allow fold-away appliances to be integrated into your own choice of cabinet or drawer units.

SPACE DIVIDERS

AREAS OF PRIVACY can be achieved in a single living space by cleverly using screening devices. Draped translucent fabric, blinds, sliding or opening panels, and simple folding screens are the traditional methods. Mobile storage units offer a flexible approach to dividing spaces, while remote-controlled aluminum venetian blinds add a dramatic high-tech touch.

MULTIPURPOSE ROOM DIVIDERS

Screens and panels make excellent room dividers but, when using them in a limited space, be sure to make the most of both sides: the front and back can be treated in different ways, either decoratively or as a support for shelving, cabinets, or clothes racks.

△ SLIDING DOORS
Sliding doors and panels take up less space than double or folding doors. These top-hung panels, which are fitted from top to bottom with shelves to maximize their use, glide together to block off the work space on the far side.

"SCREENROBE" ▷
Today's designers are producing inventive solutions to the problems of small-space living, such as this dual-purpose, cherry-wood armoire with maple-veneered MDF (medium-density fiberboard) doors and hinged side screens. In this version, two units – one with shelves and the other with hanging space – stand together; the folding panels at either side can be opened to create a simple screen, or closed and folded flat against the cabinet.

ARMOIRE
With the screens closed, the unit is an armoire with ample shelving and storage space.

SCREEN
With the side panels open and wardrobe doors closed, a solid screen is formed.

REMEMBER

■ Do not block any natural light sources when positioning screens or dividers: light is vital for creating a pleasant living environment in a small space.

■ To make the most of limited space, use both sides of a room divider, either decoratively or for functional purposes.

■ A sliding door or panel takes up much less space than either folding or double doors, and can be fitted with shelves or hooks for hanging storage.

■ Translucent drapes of muslin or silk can create a simple yet elegant room divider.

HANGING RAIL
A movable rail can be pulled to the outside of the wardrobe behind the screen, providing useful hanging space and a dressing area.

HINGED PANELS
The side panels are hinged to open outward, and to fold flat against the sides of the wardrobe.

EASY MOVING
A vertically sliding leg allows the screen panel to be positioned on an uneven surface.

SCREENS AND BLINDS

There are many ways of creating screens: Japanese-style sliding screens and natural bamboo blinds can form space-saving room dividers, while reflective aluminum slatted blinds offer a stylish alternative. Translucent materials, including fabrics such as muslin or silk, plastics, glass bricks, and sandblasted glass, are ideal for allowing light into internal spaces without loss of privacy.

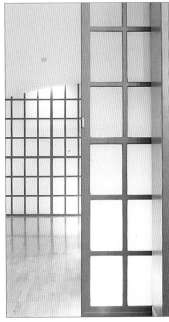

◁ HIGH-TECH SCREEN
This remote-controlled aluminum venetian blind is one of several used to divide the space in a loft apartment. The screen is light and reflective, so the interior space created by it does not appear to be boxed in.

TRANSLUCENT
SCREENING ▽
It is important, in one-room living, to maintain a sense of space and light, and this is achieved here by using a translucent screen to separate what might otherwise remain a dark understairs area.

△ MAXIMIZING LIGHT
Sandblasted glass is an attractive option for fixed and sliding screens. It makes the most of the available natural light by subtle transmission and diffusion and also permits the creation of ever-changing patterns of light and shadow, which help to enliven flat surfaces.

Storage

Order in the home relies on an efficient, well-organized storage system. Modular units, which can be acquired gradually and arranged according to individual taste and changing needs, are particularly useful, while hanging storage can be used to fill awkward spaces. Storage ranged along an entire wall can, surprisingly, create rather than reduce space.

Wall-Mounted Units

In small apartments it is essential to fit storage on the walls as far as possible in order to free floor space for general living. Wall systems range from pockets and adjustable shelves to peg-boards, brackets, and butcher's hooks, and they can be fit onto any available wall space using the appropriate attachments.

◁ Wall-Hung Rack
Vertical storage racks are practical and space-saving and can be fixed at any height, in any area of the room. This letter rack was designed for office use but it is equally suited to the storage of magazines and correspondence at home.

Vertical Storage
Made in natural plywood with steel rods, this rack is suitable for any narrow wall space.

Adjustable Shelves
The shelves on this unit can be moved up and down the pillar. They are suitable for a narrow wall space.

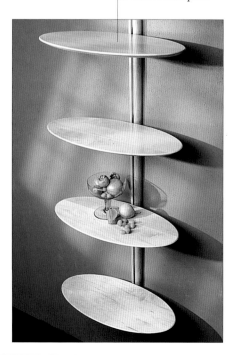

Wall-Hung
Shelving Unit ▷
For maximum flexibility look for adjustable, wall-hung shelving units such as these practical and decorative maplewood shelves, which can be easily moved up and down the single, wall-mounted pillar.

Stacking Systems

When space is limited, modular stacking units provide a neat solution to storage problems. Whether you opt for the simple method of piling matching boxes, baskets, tins, or crates on top of each other, or invest in a customized unit to suit the space available and your particular storage requirements, stacking systems provide one of the most efficient ways of fitting the maximum amount of storage into even the most restricted space.

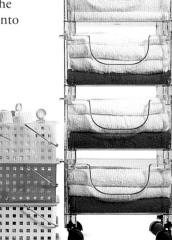

Inexpensive Crates
These plastic crates provide a practical way to store linen and towels as well as items that need ventilation.

Plastic Containers ▷
Plastic storage units range from inexpensive stacking crates to mobile trolley units with plastic trays that can be added on as required. These offer a flexible method of storing anything from clothing to household supplies.

FLEXIBLE FABRIC STORAGE

Hanging wardrobes are just one of the wide and ingenious range of storage containers made from cotton or canvas. Many of these products are ideal for small-space living: they are inexpensive, adaptable in their use, and they can be fit into odd corners. Fabric wall pockets and hanging "shelves" are particularly useful for storing small items in an organized way.

△ BASKET STORAGE
Wicker baskets are available in various sizes and provide a light, inexpensive, and portable method of storage that suits interiors with a natural, homey feel.

▽ SPACE-SAVING SYSTEM
Components of this type of metal system can be bought separately and assembled to suit your needs. The whole arrangement can be open or fit into a cabinet.

△ CANVAS SELF-ASSEMBLY CLOSETS
Easily assembled, both of these wardrobes are made of canvas. One, on a steel frame, is zip-fronted; the other has a plastic frame and roll-up front, with a floor-level shelf for shoes.

HANGING POCKETS △
A set of twelve cotton pockets, attached to a door, wall, or cupboard, can be used to store anything from scarves and gloves to cleaning equipment or shoes.

CANVAS SHELVES △
Simple and versatile, these space-saving, hanging canvas shelves for shoes, sweaters, and underwear are simply attached to the rail with a sturdy Velcro fastening.

REMEMBER

■ Stackability is the guiding principle when looking for storage containers.

■ Choose storage units in a style and finish appropriate to the space. Natural materials like bamboo and cotton possess a timeless quality, while plastics add a splash of intense color.

■ Salvage sturdy, secondhand cabinets from offices and shops. Spray with a coat of paint and attach new handles.

■ Look for flexible, modular systems that allow units to be fit into awkward spaces.

BUILT-IN STORAGE

To be successful, built-in storage should merge unobtrusively into the structure of the interior. The first task is to locate all unused spaces. If your room has high ceilings, consider constructing a false, suspended ceiling that will provide a large "attic" space; in the same way, useful underfloor storage can be created by raising the floor level. False walls, lined with shelving and cabinets, can hold a vast amount of storage, especially if teamed with pull-out fittings.

CELLAR SPACE
Opening this hatch reveals that the below-floor space has become a "cellar" holding a large amount of long-term storage.

UNDERFLOOR SPACE ▷
The construction of a raised platform or false floor can create, at the same time, new areas of storage space. In this example, storage has even been incorporated into the step leading from one floor level to another.

TOOL CHEST
The space below this step, leading from one floor level to the next, is not wasted, but forms an easily accessible tool chest.

△ BUILT-IN DRESSING ROOM
As well as a useful laundry chute and a vanity cabinet, this brightly painted built-in closet, adjacent to a raised sleeping area, contains a vertical shoe rack and a pull-out clothes hanging rail.

REMEMBER

■ As far as possible, use "dead" and wasted space, especially narrow "in-between" spaces, corners, underfloor areas, and even underneath stair treads.

■ Unused wall space above toilets, along corridors, in entrance foyers, and above windows can all be usefully fitted with storage.

■ Pack items for long-term storage in dustproof containers and ensure that environmental conditions are suitable.

■ Attic space is particularly valuable for storing possessions on a long-term basis.

WALL-TO-WALL STORAGE ▷
One of the best uses of space is to line an entire wall with a built-in storage unit. Not only can it hold all your possessions and keep the floor clear, but it also makes the interior appear larger.

△ **Integral Shelf Storage**
A vast quantity of books and boxes is stored in these shelves, which have been built in alongside the steps leading to a raised area in a loft apartment. Painted bright yellow, they look like one neat storage unit.

Long-Term Storage

Make use of high-level spaces for the long-term storage of infrequently used items, such as seasonal clothes and do-it-yourself equipment, and consider whether you need to provide permanently fixed access or a ladder that can be put away when not in use. If you are planning to remodel a room, this is an ideal opportunity to anticipate your needs and build in as much storage space as possible.

Handy Stool
When folded away, these steps double as a useful stool.

Easy Steps
The two steps pivot smoothly out from under the stool.

△ **Foldaway Steps**
Dual-purpose steps such as these, which double as a stool or side table, are useful in a small studio. Library steps that turn into a chair are a more traditional version.

Storage Heights

Use the highest level of storage for items that are rarely used.

Store items that are used regularly no higher than you can reach comfortably without steps.

Store heavy and bulky items at the lower levels.

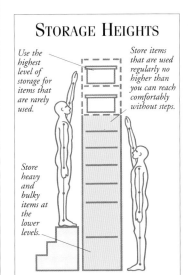

Store heavy objects at low level, and label boxes on high-level shelves with listed contents to avoid unnecessary searching.

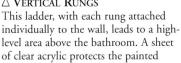

△ **Vertical Rungs**
This ladder, with each rung attached individually to the wall, leads to a high-level area above the bathroom. A sheet of clear acrylic protects the painted wall from scuff marks.

△ **High-Level Storage**
Loft space in an adjacent corridor is reached through a trap-door in the living area of this apartment, with a ladder providing the means of access.

FLOORING

THE CHOICE OF FLOORING can completely transform a room, but your decision must encompass practical considerations, such as cost and the extent of use in different areas, as well as personal style preferences. Lofts tend to feature hard finishes – exposed brick, concrete, and timber floors – which increase sound levels, but these can be muted by adding rugs and other soft materials. Underfloor heating, which is currently enjoying a revival, is compatible with most types of floor coverings, but is particularly efficient with ceramic, stone, and very well seasoned hardwood.

TEXTURED RUBBER

Available as sheet or tiles, natural or synthetic (or a blend of the two), rubber is both hard-wearing and decorative.

ADVANTAGES
• Durable and easy to clean.
• Quiet, resilient, and nonskid.
• Exciting range of colors, effects, and patterns.

DISADVANTAGES
• Shows scratches, although they can disappear.
• Dark scuff marks can be obvious.

FLOORING AS A ROOM DIVIDER
A change of color and texture is an effective way of defining two different areas in a single space.

COLOR-WASHED WOOD

Wood has its own charm, but a soft paint wash can brighten weathered boards or mask poor-quality wood.

ADVANTAGES
• You control the color depth and tone.
• Color can be reapplied at any time.
• Compatible with underfloor heating.

DISADVANTAGES
• Expands in reaction to water and humidity.
• Is not impact-resistant and can splinter.
• Tends to amplify sound levels.

ASSESS YOUR FLOORING NEEDS

■ Do you want to visually separate each living area or would you prefer the whole interior to form one spatial flow? Use flooring finishes to achieve different effects.

■ Are you planning neutral-coloured walls to create a feeling of space? A natural-colored floor will help add warmth.

■ Would you like to create space by dispensing with visible radiators? Underfloor heating provides an alternative, but check that flooring is suitable.

■ Does the luxury of walking on carpet appeal to you? If so, have you considered how much cleaning and maintenance it requires, and whether it is practical in all areas?

■ Do you like the clean lines of wooden flooring? Remember that real wood can be replaced by remarkably convincing vinyl or laminate.

■ If you like plain-colored flooring, have you considered that it shows up marks more quickly than a patterned surface?

TEXTURED VINYL

Sheet vinyl is tough, waterproof, and nonskid, and is available in a wide range of colors and textures.

ADVANTAGES
• Feels warm and absorbs sound.
• Durable and requires minimal maintenance.
• Easy to cut around awkwardly shaped walls.

DISADVANTAGES
• May be marked by furniture without casters.
• Can be stained by shoe polish and fiber pens.

NATURAL FIBER MATTING

Plant-fiber matting, such as seagrass, coir, sisal, or jute, offers a warm, natural look; it can be laid loose or wall-to-wall.

ADVANTAGES
• Hard-wearing and sound-absorbent.
• Decorative weaves and colors available.
• A natural alternative to carpet and synthetics.

DISADVANTAGES
• Borders must be bound to prevent fraying.
• Not suitable for kitchens or in direct sunlight.

WOOD LAMINATE

Made from pressed, resin-impregnated papers, laminates offer an immense variety of colors, patterns, and texture.

ADVANTAGES
• Extremely hard-wearing and durable.
• Stain-resistant, and easy to maintain.
• Designs and grain patterns do not fade.

DISADVANTAGES
• Hard surface can be noisy.
• More difficult to repair than carpet or vinyl.

VINYL TILES

With all the advantages of sheet vinyl, vinyl tiles are available in a range of colors and can look good anywhere.

ADVANTAGES
• Spare tiles can be kept to repair worn areas.
• You can create your own unique pattern.
• Tiles are quick and easy to lay.

DISADVANTAGES
• Corners may break if not stuck down firmly.
• May not be waterproof if edges are not close.
• Can be stained by waxes and solvents.

CARPET

Carpeting varies from expensive wool mixtures to cheaper synthetic blends, but all offer great comfort underfoot.

ADVANTAGES
• Range of finishes from velvet to shag pile.
• Unlimited choice of colors and patterns.
• Damaged carpet can be easily replaced.

DISADVANTAGES
• Regular cleaning needed to prolong carpet life.
• May need periodical restretching.
• Synthetic fibers react badly to burns.

LINOLEUM

Made from almost 100% natural raw materials, linoleum is tough, durable, flexible, and easily maintained.

ADVANTAGES
• A good insulator for airborne sound.
• Comfortable to stand on, with a slight "give."
• Very hygienic and resistant to bacterial growth.

DISADVANTAGES
• Can react to excessive water spills and seepage.
• Has a natural oily odor, which fades with time.
• Chairs must have soft casters.

LIGHTING

LIGHTING CAN BE DRAMATIC OR SUBTLE. It can draw the eye toward a particular focus or make parts of a room disappear. Even a dimmer switch can completely alter an interior space. The ideal is a balance between ambient and task lighting, but lights should always be selected with a specific function in mind, and knowing their effect on surrounding surfaces and materials. The days of the single, central hanging bulb are long gone, and a stream of exciting, adaptable systems offer scope for imaginative ideas for shaping space and providing a good level of visibility.

FLOORSTANDING LAMP

The universal joint connecting the arm to the support of this simple, elegant lamp provides maximum flexibility.

ADVANTAGES
• Light can be directed to where it is needed.
• Height and angle of light are easily adjusted.
• Ideal as a floorstanding reading light.

DISADVANTAGES
• Light is not easily directed upward.
• Trailing cord can be hazardous.

COMBINATION OF LIGHTING
A variety of lights, including uplights, ceiling lights, and wall-mounted spots, define different areas.

ARCHITECT-TYPE LAMP

Precisely balanced, either on a cast metal base or clamped to a work surface, this lamp is designed to rest in any position.

ADVANTAGES
• Ideal task light for working or reading.
• Can be angled to cast a pool of light.
• Very safe, weighty, cast metal base.

DISADVANTAGES
• Nuts holding light in position may loosen.
• The cord must be kept safely out of the way.
• Shade can become hot after lengthy use.

ASSESS YOUR LIGHTING NEEDS

■ Make built-in lighting an important part of your layout at the planning stage so that the electrical wiring system can be arranged before you start decorating. Outlets can then be added for lamps and lighting effects.

■ List any special features or objects that you would like to have illuminated, such as a collection of glass or prints. Make another list of kitchen cabinets, armoires, or storage spaces that will need internal lighting. Make sure that food preparation areas are adequately lit.

■ Steps and entrances and access to raised platforms must be properly lit. Lights need not be wall- or ceiling-hung, but can be mounted at low levels so that the focus of illumination is on the stair-treads.

■ If your bed doubles as seating during the day, consider flexible lighting that will be suitable for both situations. Adjustable, architect-type lights, and clip-on, extending, and floorstanding lights are all adaptable and provide a good level of task lighting.

PENDANT

The functional simplicity of this lamp fits in well with contemporary styling, and in particular with open-plan living.

ADVANTAGES
• Casts a cozy, warm pool of light onto a table.
• Height can be adjusted to suit.
• Helps to create a focal point in the room.

DISADVANTAGES
• Requires a translucent bulb to avoid dazzle.
• Position of dining table is limited.

CLIP-ON WORK LAMP

This flexible lamp, originally designed for photography studios, has now been adapted to suit any part of the home.

ADVANTAGES
• Can be clipped to any suitable spot.
• Can provide ambient uplighting.
• Suitable as a bedside or countertop light.

DISADVANTAGES
• Trailing cord can be dangerous.
• Clip can mark wooden furniture.

WALL-HUNG UPLIGHT

Uplights throw soft, reflected light around a room, creating ideal ambient lighting for living areas and relaxing.

ADVANTAGES
• Can enhance architectural features.
• Translucent shade produces diffused light.
• Bulb and wiring are concealed.

DISADVANTAGES
• Electrical wiring must be concealed.
• Not suitable for reading or working.

MINI DOWNLIGHTERS

Low-voltage halogen fittings are now so small that they can be totally concealed in recesses on the underside of a shelf.

ADVANTAGES
• Are totally hidden and do not dazzle.
• Create bright, even lighting on worktops.
• Not hot enough to damage shelving.

DISADVANTAGES
• Difficult to conceal the wiring.
• A position has to be found for the transformer.
• Gloves needed to handle the bulbs.

BARE-WIRE SYSTEM

Mini low-voltage halogen spotlights rest on parallel tensile wires, which act as the track between two points.

ADVANTAGES
• Lights can be easily moved along the cables.
• Halogen light has minimal effect on colors.
• Light can be directed onto a countertop.

DISADVANTAGES
• Transformer needed to convert electric current.
• Light can create glare.
• Transformer must be installed by an electrician.

EXTENDING LIGHT

Both practical and decorative, an extending light can provide a high level of light without causing eyestrain.

ADVANTAGES
• Light can be directed where needed.
• Lamp can be retracted when not in use.
• Can be angled to create a wash of light.

DISADVANTAGES
• Lamp will not stay in position if fittings loosen.
• Cord difficult to conceal.
• Clinical design may not suit all interiors.

ROOM PLANS

LINEAR ROOM PLAN

THE 50-FOOT LONG INTERIOR SPACE in this late-nineteenth-century London interior allows the main functional areas to relate in one continuous and logical flow. The separate parts are defined by different floor finishes – sisal, antique Persian carpet, chequered vinyl, and natural wood – as well as by a progression of wall colors and finishes, including cool white and rich red paintwork, natural wood, and glass.

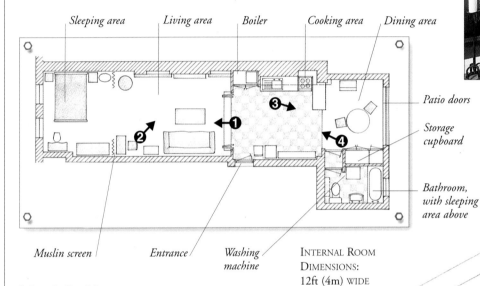

Sleeping area · Living area · Boiler · Cooking area · Dining area

Patio doors

Storage cupboard

Bathroom, with sleeping area above

Muslin screen · Entrance · Washing machine

INTERNAL ROOM DIMENSIONS:
12ft (4m) WIDE
50ft (16m) LONG

△ BIRD'S-EYE VIEW
The linear layout is a planner's dream: each of the functional areas is self-contained and distinct from its neighbor, yet forms part of the general flow.

NO WASTED SPACE
Floor-to-ceiling shelving for books and other objects makes the best possible use of the available space.

△ ❶ DRAMATIC DRAPERY
The dramatic view from the richly decorated living area toward the tranquil "bedroom" is framed by muslin drapes. These help define and screen the sleeping area, and create a calm and luminous effect in the morning light.

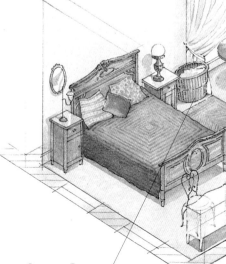

STORAGE BASKETS
Wicker baskets provide versatile storage for bed linens or laundry and complement the antique furnishings.

TRANSLUCENT SCREENING
Filmy white muslin provides an inexpensive but highly effective method of screening the sleeping area without any loss of light.

◁ **❷ HEARTH AND HOME**
An artificial fire, cushions, and shelves crammed with books and other treasured possessions create an inviting and homey focus to the living area.

LIGHT AND SPACE
An entirely glazed end wall fills the dining area with light and adds to the sense of space.

HIDDEN UTILITIES
Louvered doors on floor-to-ceiling cabinets neatly conceal the boiler and essential cleaning equipment.

❸ WEST-FACING WINDOW ▷
The west-facing end wall is entirely glazed, filling the apartment with light for the best part of the day and giving the illusion of the interior flowing out to the wood-decked roof terrace. A window-cleaner's ladder provides access to the high-level bed alcove.

GUEST ROOM
A platform above the bathroom area is large enough to hold a king-size bed and benefits from the natural light source.

FOR MORE DETAILS...

Muslin drapes as room dividers SEE P. *10*

Changing floor levels SEE P. *10*

Link to outdoors SEE P. *13*

Access to high-level storage SEE P. *43*

Floor coverings SEE PP. *44–45*

LAUNDRY FACILITY
A washing machine fits conveniently into a corner of the bathroom.

STORAGE CABINET
Space reclaimed from the bathroom area under the platform provides useful storage

ISLAND BAR
A simple bar serves as work surface, snack counter, and natural break between the kitchen and dining areas.

ENTRANCE
The only entrance to the apartment leads directly into the kitchen area from the communal hallway of the building.

CHANGING LEVELS
The raised kitchen floor level physically separates the cooking and living spaces.

❹ UNINTERRUPTED SPACE ▷
For those living in one room, linear interior space has the practical advantage of permitting easy, unimpeded movement. Equally importantly, a long view through to a garden or roof terrace helps dispel any feelings of claustrophobia that may be created by living in a confined area.

DESIGN POINTS

■ When space is limited, a building's aspect is particularly important in terms of light: an east/west facing house, for example, enjoys light all day.

■ When planning the layout, analyze your lifestyle closely to help achieve a smooth flow for everyday activities.

■ Retain original architectural features and incorporate them into your plan. For example, you may consider filling the alcoves on either side of a chimney with shelving.

■ Don't waste space, no matter how small, oddly shaped, or unconventional. The most unlikely places can usually hold items for storage.

■ Position a sleeping platform near a top-opening window so that the area has its own source of natural light and ventilation.

LINEAR ROOM CHOICE

△ UNIFIED SPACE
Although the separate sleeping, cooking, and dining areas in this restricted living space are divided by cabinets, shelves, and a solid wall, the white paintwork and single type of flooring throughout help unify the interior and prevent any feelings of claustrophobia.

SPACE AND LIGHT ▷
The double-height window, toward which the living and sleeping areas are oriented, links the interior with the exterior, bathing the former with light. White paint, upholstery, and linen help reflect the light around the apartment and enhance the feeling of free-flowing space, which is unimpeded by screens or partitions.

△ ROOM IN A GARDEN
The entire end wall of the kitchen area has been transformed into a glazed conservatory, cleverly integrating the garden and the interior, while a curved island worktop with inset sink and drainer takes advantage of the natural light and panoramic garden view to create a pleasant workplace.

△ DEFINING SPACE
Semitransparent materials add an interesting texture to walls and dividers. As well as acting as a screen and creating a sense of privacy, they permit light to be filtered through and draw the eye to the space beyond. In this interior, rugs laid at right angles also help define different areas.

△ DIVIDING A LARGE SPACE
The scale of this former industrial interior could be overwhelming but, by placing a sofa against a paneled wall at right angles to the dining area and installing a bamboo blind to screen off the entrance, comfortable divisions have been created without losing the overall flow of space.

COMPACT ROOM PLAN

TWO ROOMS ON THE GROUND FLOOR of a small town house have been transformed into a studio space that, despite occupying only about 450 square feet (42 square meters), gives an overall impression of light and space. The carefully considered color treatment of surfaces in the kitchen is enhanced by the otherwise white interior, as are the collections of colored glassware displayed in the studio.

INTERNAL ROOM DIMENSIONS:
16ft (5m) WIDE
29ft (9m) LONG

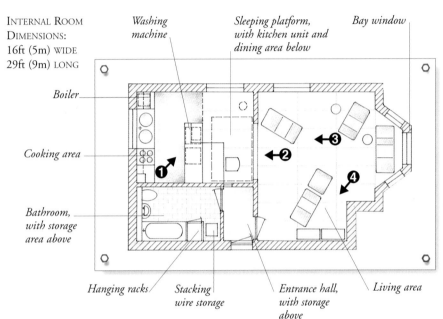

Washing machine

Sleeping platform, with kitchen unit and dining area below

Bay window

Boiler

Cooking area

Bathroom, with storage area above

Hanging racks

Stacking wire storage

Entrance hall, with storage above

Living area

SHARED WINDOW
One window is shared between the living area below and the sleeping platform above.

△ BIRD'S-EYE VIEW
Parts of the original dividing wall remain, but the effect is of a single space, with the advantage of natural light from three sides. Although functional areas have been reduced to a minimum, there is no loss of comfort.

DESIGN POINTS

■ Whenever possible, try to construct a sleeping platform alongside a window to ensure good ventilation and a source of natural light.

■ Even in a very small living area, it should be possible to find space to display collections of objects; look especially at any tall, narrow gaps.

■ A simple worktop and a pair of folding or stacking trestles provide a work surface or a dining table for entertaining guests and can be stored unobtrusively until required.

■ Check with an architect on fixed structural features, then look for imaginative ways of incorporating them into your overall plan.

△ ❶ PLATFORM ABOVE THE KITCHEN
The ceiling is about 10 feet (3 meters) high, allowing for a sleeping platform large enough to hold a television and books by the bed. Natural light and ventilation are provided by a window shared with the area below.

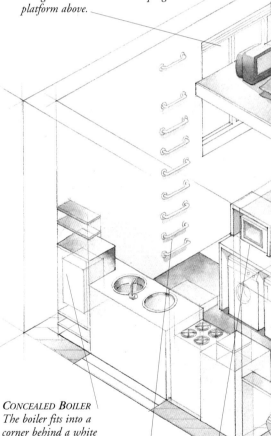

CONCEALED BOILER
The boiler fits into a corner behind a white cupboard front.

SPACE-SAVING LADDER
Sturdy rungs, originally from a ships' chandler, provide access to the sleeping platform.

CUSTOM-MADE UNIT
A washing machine, microwave, refrigerator, and vegetable rack are all housed in a custom-made unit.

◁ ❷ OCCASIONAL DINING FURNITURE
When a dining space is needed, the work surface
is folded away and a dining table assembled from
a simple table-top and trestles, which are easily
stored, along with the stacking chairs, when not
in use. The kitchen unit conceals a refrigerator,
washing machine, and microwave oven.

WINDOW FEATURE
Original large bay
window provides
natural light that is
reflected throughout
the interior.

MODULAR SEATING
Foam seating units
interlock to double
as a spare bed when
required.

VERTICAL LIGHTING
A 1970s Italian
lamp runs on a cable
from ceiling to floor
through a hole in
the platform.

△ ❸ INSTANT WORK STATION
A simple work station is quickly assembled by
lifting the horizontally hinged table-top and
supporting it on another panel, which is
hung vertically. When not in use, the panels
fold unobtrusively against the kitchen unit,
which not only provides a useful shelf, but
also screens off much of the cooking area.

FOR MORE DETAILS...

Modular foam furniture
SEE P. 20

Stacking chairs SEE P. 29

Hinged work station
SEE PP. 30–31

FLEXIBLE SHELVING
A modular shelving system,
here packed with books, CDs,
and audio equipment, can be
added to as necessary.

STORAGE SPACE
A hatch leads to storage
space above the entrance
foyer and bathroom.

ENTRANCE
Access to the apartment from the
communal hallway is via a foyer,
which also houses shoe storage.

COMPACT BATHROOM
The bathroom has just enough
room for a bath with shower,
toilet, and sink.

MINIMAL CLOSET
Two hanging racks, one above the
other, and a mobile stack of wire
baskets constitute the closet.

△ ❹ MODULAR STORAGE RACK
Storage of books, magazines, telephone/fax machine,
and mini sound system, is all contained within a
modular metal rack system along one wall.

COMPACT ROOM CHOICE

△ **KITCHEN IN A CABINET**
An imaginative variation on the kitchen-in-a-cabinet theme is
to recycle a secondhand armoire. Here, a small sink has been
plumbed in, with shelving and drawers underneath. Tiling
and shelves complete this neat, hideaway unit.

△ **REMODELED ROOM**
A deep, false wall provides a practical way of creating a room
within a room. Here, above a large amount of storage space
and a doorway, a spacious bedroom has been created, the
whole structure lightened by being painted completely white.

△ **CORNER KITCHEN**
A compact kitchen, with a sink,
small stove, and hood, has been fit
into this corner, with practical
suspended shelving above.

COLOR COORDINATION ▷
Many space-creating features, such
as a convertible sofabed, folding
chairs, and a glass-topped table, are
demonstrated in this small studio,
which also illustrates the way in
which color can be used to enhance
the sense of space.

OPEN-PLAN ROOM PLAN

METICULOUS PLANNING along strong horizontal axes gives this studio, which measures only 17 x 28 feet (5 x 8.5 meters), a feeling of calm spaciousness despite its busy urban location. The functional areas are defined by varying floor levels and by boxed-in vertical supports, but the horizontal flow of space is maintained, with no view being blocked by a full-height wall.

Living and dining area Work area Rails for bed Bamboo blinds Bed, with sunken bath beneath

INTERNAL ROOM DIMENSIONS:
17ft (5m) WIDE
28ft (8.5m) LONG

Armoire

Sleeping area

Vanity unit built into remodeled wall

Boiler

Cooking area Washing machine Toilet and utility area Entrance foyer Access to under-floor storage.

FOR MORE DETAILS...

Bath under bed SEE PP. 32–33

Foldaway ironing table SEE P. 37

Underfloor storage SEE P. 42

△ BIRD'S-EYE VIEW
A vast amount of concealed storage space has been planned into this apartment, as well as an ingenious, double-function sleeping and washing area.

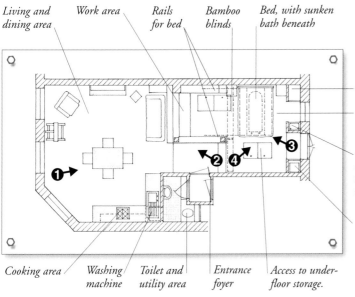

DUAL-PURPOSE TABLETOP
A folded tabletop extension, which fits over the dining table, makes up the front of this storage cabinet.

ARTISTIC FOCUS
An artist's easel provides a clue to the interests enjoyed by the occupant of this apartment.

◁ ❶ UNBROKEN VIEW
The dining area is located at the junction of the two major axes, accentuating the length of the interior. Since no solid wall interrupts the view, the sitting, working, cooking, and sleeping areas are all visible.

FLEXIBLE SEATING
When not in use, these lightweight folding metal chairs with wooden slats can be easily stored.

◁❷ RAISED WORK STATION
The centrally placed work area is on a raised
level that not only separates it from the living
and dining areas, but also provides extensive
underfloor storage space.

SCREENING OPTIONS
*Two bamboo blinds screen off either
the sleeping/washing area or the
entire end section of the studio.*

STUDY AREA
*A large bookshelf
along the side wall
emphasizes the
horizontal
accent.*

UNDERBED STORAGE
*Although the bed
contains large, built-
in storage drawers, it
can be easily rolled
over the sunken bath.*

VANITY UNIT
*A small sink and
cabinet are concealed
in the remodeled
end wall.*

△❸ NATURAL LIGHTING
The interior of the apartment is illuminated by
reflected light from windows at both ends of the
room, although privacy in the bathing and sleeping
area can be created by lowering the bamboo blinds.

CONCEALED BOILER
*Hidden in the remodeled
wall is a combination boiler,
which obviates the need for
a bulky hot water tank.*

UNDERFLOOR STORAGE
*Marine-style hatches give
access to long-term storage
space beneath the raised
wood flooring.*

BUILT-IN TOOL CHEST
*The stair-tread lifts up to
reveal additional storage
space that is ideal for tools.*

DEAD SPACE
*A washing machine, accessed
from the bathroom/utility room,
fills the otherwise inaccessible
space in the kitchen unit.*

FOLDAWAY IRONING BOARD
*An extending ironing board
occupies minimal space in the
kitchen unit.*

❹ JAPANESE-STYLE BATHROOM ▷
A spacious bathroom is created by lowering the
blinds and rolling back the bed to reveal the
sunken bath. The remodeled end wall contains
an armoire, cabinets, and vanity unit.

DESIGN POINTS

■ Create a sense of warmth
and cohesion in an open-plan
interior by choosing natural
materials such as wood,
bamboo, and plain cotton.

■ Forget tradition when fitting
plumbed-in equipment: it may
be cheaper to take the machine
to the plumbing rather than
the plumbing to the machine.

■ To increase a sense of space
and avoid claustrophobia, limit
dividing walls to half height.

■ Vary floor levels to create
spatial variety and to provide
underfloor storage space.

■ Avoid condensation in a
windowless internal bath area
by installing a fan.

OPEN-PLAN ROOM CHOICE

△ HALF-WALL DIVIDER
The upstand at the back of this kitchen counter successfully separates the preparation and cooking areas from the main living space, without blocking them off entirely.

◁ UNDERFLOOR STORAGE
Constructing a new, raised floor level is a way of creating a room within a room, as well as providing a large amount of useful and easily accessible long-term storage space.

△ SPACE-DEFINING DEVICES
Functional areas are defined here by devices such as blinds, half-height walls, and different floor levels. The bathroom is visually separated, with minimal privacy, but remains part of the main living area.

HIGH-LEVEL READING AREA ▷
If ceiling height permits, the construction of a gallery releases living space. Here, a library above a bank of roomy cabinets has been created. Painted white, they merge successfully into the general structure.

LARGE ROOM PLAN

WITH THE ORIGINAL TILING RESTORED and the aggregate pillars and ducting left exposed, the industrial aesthetic is retained in this loft in a converted riverside warehouse. The effect is softened, however, by the use of color and the introduction of antique furniture. As the ceiling is not high enough to construct another floor, a galleried work area has been created above a bank of built-in kitchen cabinets.

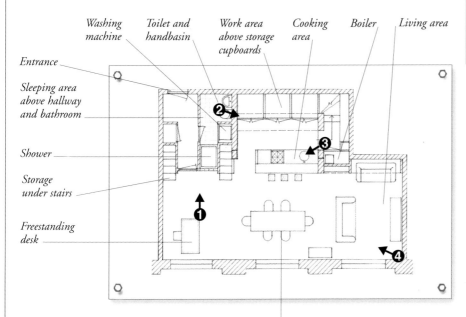

Washing machine — Toilet and handbasin — Work area above storage cupboards — Cooking area — Boiler — Living area

Entrance —

Sleeping area above hallway and bathroom —

Shower —

Storage under stairs —

Freestanding desk —

Dining area

BIRD'S-EYE VIEW △
Three large windows, providing a view of the river and a source of natural light, are a major feature in this loft and formed the main influence on the plan, which packs all services against the inner wall.

INTERNAL ROOM DIMENSIONS:
24ft (7m) WIDE
36ft (11m) LONG

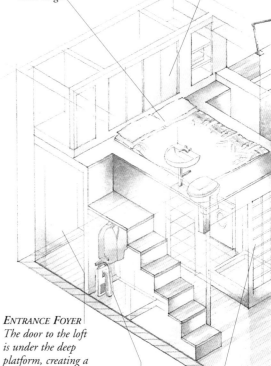

BUILT-IN CLOSET
Along the back wall, a built-in closet and cabinets are painted a cheery bright yellow.

PLATFORM BED
The bed is sunk into the platform and surrounded by a wide ledge.

ENTRANCE FOYER
The door to the loft is under the deep platform, creating a dramatic entrance.

UNDERSTAIRS STORAGE
In the entrance hall, under the stairs, is a space for coats and cleaning equipment.

SHOWER CUBICLE
Alongside the utility area is a large shower with natural light transmitted through glass bricks.

FOR MORE DETAILS...

Workstation with glazed panels SEE P. 11

Glass brick panel in internal shower-room SEE P. 12

Built-in shelves lining entire wall SEE PP. 42–43

◁ **❶ COLORFUL ENTRANCE**
Above the entrance to the loft is a symmetrically planned sleeping platform with built-in closets behind. The bathroom, utility area, and shower cubicle are underneath, with natural light entering through the glass brick wall. Two sets of deep steps conceal long-term storage.

◁ ❷ HIGH-LEVEL WORK STATION

The long work desk, which has been built on a raised platform above the walk-in kitchen cupboards, offers an overall view of the loft interior and of the river, as well as providing a quiet work space that is separate yet still part of the whole.

❸ DUAL-PURPOSE BREAKFAST BAR ▷

The food preparation and washing-up areas are screened by an oak upstand that functions as both a breakfast bar and a space divider. The bar is fitted with small strip lights that give a decorative effect as well as useful illumination.

WALL OF STORAGE
Bookshelves, holding magazines, books, and storage boxes, have been put into one entire wall of the loft.

INDOOR GARDEN
A plant shelf introduces a natural element to the industrial scale of the loft space.

EXTRA LIGHT
Sandblasted glazing panels along the lower front of the desk allow light into the darkest part of the work platform.

PANTRIES
Capacious walk-in pantries contain a microwave and freezer as well as food and other cooking equipment.

OLD AND NEW
A large, renovated, antique armoire adds a personal touch.

DESIGN POINTS

■ When planning a loft space, aim to work with, not against, the existing structure and, if possible, try to accommodate the existing services.

■ Opt for glass bricks instead of a solid wall to allow light into a dark interior space while still preserving privacy.

■ If you work from home, try to separate the work space from the main living area.

■ Sensitively handled color is a useful device for defining function, shaping space, and providing a focus.

■ Salvaged or antique furniture adds individuality to an industrial-scale interior.

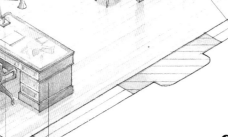

ANTIQUE DESK
An antique partners' desk, at right angles to the dining table, commands a long view of the loft.

OAK WORKTOP AND COUNTER
All the kitchen appliances are built-in behind the worktop and counter, which are made of oak – the same wood as the flooring.

❹ COLOR-CODED AREAS ▷

With the different living zones clearly color-coded – blue for the bathroom, yellow for the sleeping and work spaces, and salmon pink for the kitchen and living areas – the effect is reminiscent of an abstract Cubist interior.

LARGE ROOM CHOICE

△ DISTINCTIVE FEATURE
A sense of scale has been given to the interior by this dramatic roof truss – an original architectural feature that has been retained and incorporated into the shelves and counter. The kitchen area is defined by studded rubber flooring and screened by a sliding door that becomes part of a wall of cabinets when closed.

△ FULL-HEIGHT SCREEN
Painted in a strong color, against which red and white furniture and a collection of ceramics stand out in contrast, a blank, full-height wall screens off the kitchen area while still allowing a flow of air and space. A small painting provides a focus.

◁ SCULPTURED LIVING
In this minimalist interior, living elements – contained along one side of the loft behind blocks of built-in storage – are reduced to abstract sculptured forms. The use of soft color and a natural timber flooring averts any impression of coldness.

CREATED LIGHT AND SPACE ▷
Although this corner kitchen has no natural light source, a sense of light and spaciousness has been achieved. A glass shelf with a stainless steel hanging rack is suspended above the island bar, with additional glass and metal fixtures along the rear wall. Color has been used to define a large flat expanse of architrave.

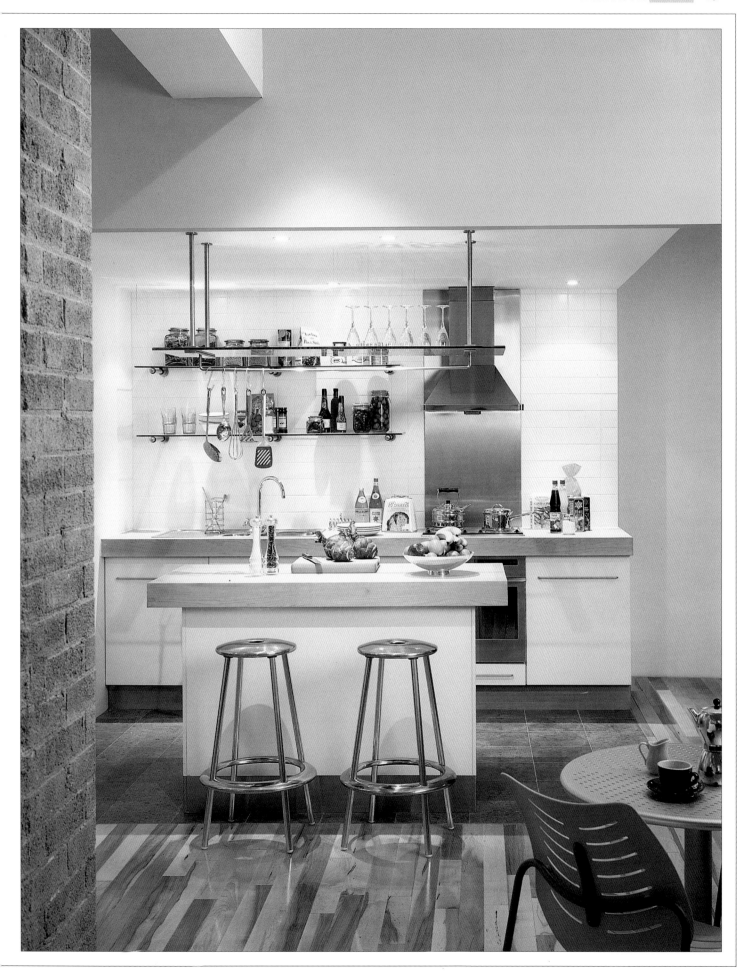

GALLERIED ROOM PLAN

ORIGINALLY BOUGHT as a bare shell in part of a redeveloped warehouse, with only basic services installed, this apartment has been created by architects specializing in loft design. The use of strong colors softens the industrial rawness of exposed ducting and brickwork, and only the bed deck, floating dramatically above the kitchen/dining section, breaks the curve of the wall containing the functional areas.

Built-in armoire, vanity, and laundry chute

Washing machine

Stairs to sleeping area

Boiler

Shower-room with raised deck above

Entrance

Shelves in narrow alcove

Built-in functional areas behind curved wall

Bed deck extends out above kitchen area

Dining area

Living area

BIRD'S-EYE VIEW △
All the service elements are tucked away behind the curved wall, leaving a clear living space that has the benefit of natural light from three windows.

INTERNAL ROOM DIMENSIONS:
15ft (4.6m) WIDE
38ft (11.6m) LONG

BED-DECK ILLUMINATION
Small spotlights are clamped at low levels to the balustrade surrounding the bed deck.

WALL OF STORAGE
The built-in storage unit, made of MDF, has a space-saving, pull-out clothes rack and shoe shelves.

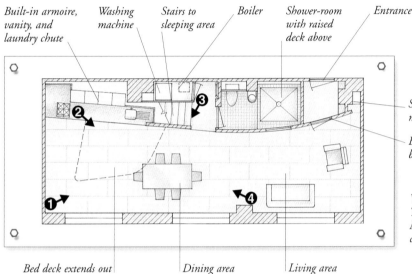

FOR MORE DETAILS...

Cooking area with suspended glass hood SEE P. 26

Shower-room SEE P. 32

Vertical ladder made from scaffold sections SEE P. 43

Built-in armoire SEE P. 42

◁ **❶ SPACIOUS LINES**
A continuous, uncluttered stretch of birch-faced plywood flooring follows the elegant line of the service wall, whose double height makes the living space appear larger. The loft height is also accentuated by light that is reflected onto the main end wall from concealed strip lighting in a narrow alcove.

EXTRACTOR HOOD
Above the stove, a suspended sheet of etched glass provides an unusual and attractive hood for the extractor ducting.

NATURAL MATERIAL
A slate countertop, with grooved drainboard, is installed over the kitchen cabinets.

◁ **❷ OVERALL VIEWS**
This is a loft with exciting perspectives in all directions: from the bed deck, beyond the wall-mounted television, the main loft space is visible. To the left, the view is of the second deck, with shower-room below.

SECONDARY DECK
A raised deck above the shower-room can be used as a guest room or for storage.

CLOTHES-CARE SOLUTION
A useful laundry chute leads to the utility area and washing machine below.

VERTICAL LADDER
Access to the raised deck is constructed from scaffold sections.

❸ CONTRASTING FEATURES ▷
Behind the facade, the warm, colorful sleeping area, reached by narrow steps, provides a contrast to the expanse of raw brickwork and large-scale original windows in this industrial space.

PERFORATED METAL SCREEN
A panel of perforated metal, spotlit from behind and "floating" in front of the wall, lets light into the deck area.

NATURAL LIGHT
Light filters into the bathroom through a frosted glass window.

REFLECTED LIGHTING
Light from the strip lighting behind these narrow vertical shelves is reflected back into the main living area.

DESIGN POINTS

■ Be sure to maintain a free flow of space in the living area if all the functional areas have to be fitted into tight quarters.

■ Color plays an important part in shaping an interior: a cool, minimalist, industrial-style loft can be humanized by an expanse of strong color.

■ An armoire or closet with pull-out bars can be fitted into a shallower space than one with a single end-to-end bar.

LUXURY SHOWER-ROOM
Although wide enough for a tub, the area is equipped with a stainless steel shower tray and an extra-large showerhead.

❹ SLEEPING BALCONY ▷
Perched on an exposed steel beam above the kitchen area is a bed deck with a balustrade of perforated aluminum. It appears like a theater balcony, lit by small spotlights, yet the deck provides a comfortable sleeping platform with built-in storage alongside.

SERVICE PANELS
Access to lighting transformers under the bed deck is provided by removable panels.

GALLERIED ROOM CHOICE

△ **VERTICAL ACCESS**
The industrial impression of a steel ladder leading up to the sleeping platform in this loft apartment is softened by the lavender paintwork.

◁ **NATURAL CHOICE**
Bamboo blinds, basketware, wood fittings, and a soft carpet provide warm natural colors and textures that harmonize with the exposed brick walls and ceiling beams.

△ **CORNER KITCHEN**
A mini kitchen has been neatly slotted into the corner beneath the narrow gallery. Boldly painted sliding doors allow the paraphernalia of plumbing, ducts, and kitchen storage to be quickly concealed from view.

RUSTIC CHARM ▷
This homey kitchen, brightened by natural light, fits neatly under a wide gallery. It illustrates the delightful effect that can be achieved by furnishing a kitchen with old items of furniture instead of matched cabinets.

LOFT PLAN

THE DISTINGUISHING FEATURE of this minimalist, high-tech loft is the use of remote-controlled, aluminum-slatted blinds to divide up the space at different times of the day, while still allowing light to filter through. The device introduces an element of fun and adds to the astonishing illusion of space created by an entire wall of mirror. All the light sources are concealed so that this studio is filled with reflected light.

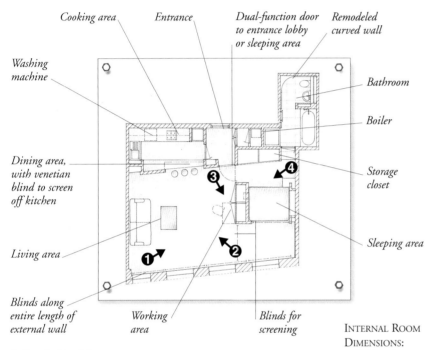

Cooking area · Entrance · Dual-function door to entrance lobby or sleeping area · Remodeled curved wall

Washing machine

Bathroom

Boiler

Dining area, with venetian blind to screen off kitchen

Storage closet

Living area

Sleeping area

Blinds along entire length of external wall · Working area · Blinds for screening

INTERNAL ROOM DIMENSIONS:
22ft (6.7m) WIDE
26ft (8.1m) LONG

△ BIRD'S-EYE VIEW
The kitchen, bathroom, and storage areas are sited along the internal wall, while the uncluttered, main living space of the loft captures the natural light flowing in from the large windows.

DESIGN POINTS

■ A series of blinds can dramatically alter an interior space, creating new areas and separating off others.

■ Mirrors are a powerful source of illusion. The larger they are, the more effective, but even a small framed mirror gives the impression of a room beyond.

■ Balance the cool effect of a minimalist, high-tech loft with the warmth of a timber floor. Parquet laid at right angles to the main axis will appear to widen an interior space.

△ ❷ KITCHEN SCREENING
With the blind lowered and the slats only partially closed, reflections from downlights play on the polished granite countertop, animating the kitchen area behind.

ALCOVE SHELVING
Shelving is tucked into a corner alcove, below a lowered ceiling with concealed lighting.

BREAKFAST BAR
A polished granite counter provides a dining bar between the kitchen and the living area.

◁ ❶ SHIMMERING REFLECTIVE WALL
The entire external wall of the loft is hung with aluminum blinds. These create a shimmering wall that is reflected in the mirrored end wall, doubling the space visually. A bright red table adds a splash of color to this cool interior.

❸ INSTANT OFFICE ▷
A small home office is quickly assembled out of the bank of storage by opening one cupboard door as a gate-leg support and dropping down another as a work surface.

KITCHEN BLIND
A blind screens off the entire kitchen and dining area.

CURVED WALL
A gently curving false wall leads the eye around.

DUAL-FUNCTION DOOR
The entrance door can be used to close off access to the bedroom and bathroom.

STORAGE BANK
A bank of cabinets provides generous storage space and screens the sleeping area.

BEDSIDE STORAGE
A useful set of narrow shelves is concealed at either side of the headboard.

CREATING SPACE
Remote-controlled venetian blinds screen the bed, creating at the same time a private or spare bedroom area.

MIRROR ILLUSION
An end wall completely filled with mirrors visually doubles the length of the studio and increases the light level.

FOR MORE DETAILS...

Curved bathroom wall
SEE P. 13

Mirrored wall SEE P. 13

Granite breakfast bar
SEE PP. 28–29

Blinds as screens SEE P. 39

FOLD-DOWN DESK
A useful home office space, created out of two cabinet fronts, is hidden from view when not in use.

❹ PRIVATE SLEEPING AREA ▷
The bed, with storage drawer underneath, is shielded by a bank of cabinets featuring a small, square, Japanese-style display cavity. By lowering a blind on the left-hand side, and swinging the entrance door around to close off the other side, a private sleeping area is created.

WALL OF BLINDS
Remote-controlled aluminum venetian blinds, covering four windows, line the entire external wall of the loft.

LOFT CHOICE

◁ TOWEL-RACK ROOM DIVIDER
Decorative in shape, color, and
finish, towel warmers are not simply
functional items. They can play an
important role in bathroom design.
A freestanding vertical panel or
ladder-style radiator, for example,
can act not just as a towel rack and
room heater but also as a room
divider in an open-plan loft space.

DIVIDING LOFT SPACE ▷
Several ways of dividing space are
illustrated in this minimalist loft.
Extra-wide folding panels can
rapidly be pulled across to conceal
the kitchen, which is built under a
gallery that divides the vertical space
at one end of the room. A panel of
translucent glazing allows light into
a private area of the gallery, while a
curved metal balustrade partially
screens the open section.

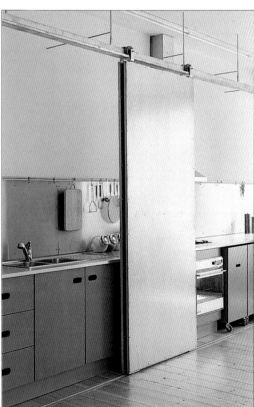

△ INDUSTRIAL SLIDING PANELS
Suspended, factory-style sliding panels offer a
high-tech alternative to folding doors and blinds
for screening off areas within a room. They take
up less space than any folding system and can be
faced with a choice of finishes, from metallic
laminate to veneer, paint, and plastics.

△ GLAZED SCREEN
A peaceful home-office space has been created
here by placing a solid white screen behind the
sofa. Above the screen is a glazed panel that
allows the light and the line of the flush wall
cabinets to flow through, following the direction
of the flooring planks.

PLOT YOUR ROOM

THE FIRST STEP IN PLANNING is to make a careful survey of your existing room so that accurate scale drawings of the floor plan and elevations can be produced. It is useful to take a series of reference photographs of the room at this stage.

COLORED PENCILS

ERASER

NOTEPAD

EQUIPMENT
To help you collect the information needed to produce an accurate record of your room's dimensions and features, you will need the basic equipment shown here.

CAMERA

TAPE MEASURE

STEPLADDER

FLOOR DIMENSIONS

You do not need to be an architect to draw a floor plan, but only accurate measurements can tell you if existing appliances and furniture will fit in your new space. Familiarize yourself with the interior, especially details such as the location of services, variations in floor level, and features that cannot be easily changed. Although professional help may be needed to deal with these (especially if plumbing or wiring have to be moved), try to begin visualizing the room as your future living space.

❶ DRAW A FLOOR PLAN
The first step in producing a floor plan is simply to draw a rough sketch of the floor area, making sure that you include features such as chimneys, alcoves, and any built-in furniture that you plan to incorporate into your new design.

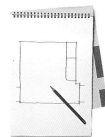

❷ MEASURE THE FLOOR
Next, measure the length and width of the floor and note the measurements on your sketch. It may be worth checking the measurements at different points, as walls are not always even. Note also the measurement of any alcoves or other features.

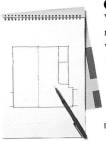

❸ PLOT WALL LENGTHS
Working around the room, measure the length of each wall, carefully noting the measurements on your sketch for future reference. You may find that the room is not symmetrical, and it is useful to know this in advance.

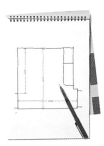

❹ NOTE SERVICE POINTS
Survey the room for service points, such as gas supply, electrical outlets, and radiators, and plot their position on your sketch. Indicate structural features such as chimney flues and outside walls, and make a note of room orientation.

❺ PLOT FIXTURES
Measure the dimensions of any built-in cabinets or shelving that you wish to retain, noting their position in the room, and adding them to your sketch. It may be fairly easy, however, to relocate such items if they are awkwardly positioned.

❻ PHOTOGRAPH ODD CORNERS
Take reference photographs to help you record areas of the room that are difficult to measure, such as awkward corners or sloping walls. Photographs of certain features will help you recall style details when you start designing your new apartment.

WALL ELEVATIONS

Detailed elevations are not necessary, but a sketch survey of all walls is useful, especially if the ceiling is high enough to allow a gallery or loft bed to be constructed. These sketches will help to establish whether there is enough wall space for furniture, without blocking windows, radiators, or other built-in features. Elevations help you imagine how your space will be when furnished.

❶ MEASURE THE HEIGHT
Stand facing each wall in turn and draw a rough sketch. Draw in doors, windows, and alcoves. Now measure the floor-to-ceiling height and note this on the sketch. Architectural features, such as moldings, are not important at this stage.

❷ MEASURE THE DOORS
On each wall sketch, record the height and width of any doors, baseboards, and cornices, plus details of any frames or moldings. Note which way the doors are hung and the position of any service points that you do not wish to obstruct.

DRAWING SCALE PLANS

Having made rough sketches, marked with accurate measurements, of your existing space *(see left)*, the next step is to draw up the scale plan and elevations on graph paper, with each square representing a set dimension. Then you can start experimenting with ideas for a multipurpose living space.

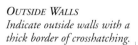

OUTSIDE WALLS
Indicate outside walls with a thick border of crosshatching.

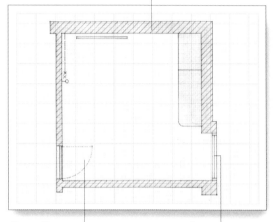

DOOR OPENING
Draw a dotted line to indicate the direction in which the door opens.

LIGHT
Parallel lines show a window as a light source.

YOU WILL NEED
Imperial and metric graph paper is supplied with this book, but you will also need a triangle, ruler, pen, pencil, pencil sharpener, and eraser.

◁**❶ TRANSFER THE FLOOR PLAN**
Plot the four perimeter walls to scale on graph paper, referring to your rough plan for precise measurements and using a triangle to draw right angles. Next, plot key features such as outside walls, doors, windows, and any changes in floor level that are important for planning your space.

CORNICE DIMENSIONS
The height of storage units will be limited by cornice size.

❷ DRAW AN ELEVATION ▷
Referring to your rough plan for measurements, draw one wall to scale. Work from the floor upward, marking on details and services last.

DOOR HANDLE
Indicate the way the door opens by drawing in the door handle.

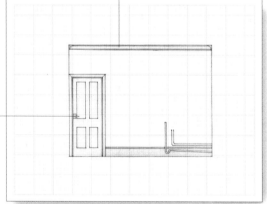

❸ OTHER ELEVATIONS ▽
Draw each of the remaining elevations to scale, marking on relevant details to give you a complete picture of the room before you begin the design.

BASEBOARD
Draw a thicker line to indicate the top of the baseboard.

WINDOWS
Include details, such as molding and windowsill measurements.

THE WHOLE PICTURE
For accuracy, draw in the radiator, baseboard, and the side of a cabinet, as seen on this elevation.

PLACE THE FEATURES

BEGIN BY COMPILING A LIST of all the furniture, appliances, and materials that you wish to include in your room, noting your preferences for where and how you like to eat, work, relax, wash, and sleep. Add to this any special hobby or storage requirements, and then you are ready to find out if your ideal living plan is possible. Place a sheet of tracing paper over the scaled-up room plan and start drawing in the basic fixtures and furniture, bearing in mind our Design Guidelines *(see right.)* You will probably draw many versions and discover unexpected possibilities before reaching the best solution.

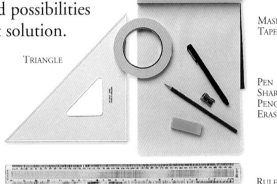

TRACING PAPER

TRIANGLE

MASKING TAPE

PEN
SHARPENER
PENCIL
ERASER

RULER

YOU WILL NEED ▷
Place a sheet of tracing paper over your floor plan scale drawing, holding them securely in position with masking tape. Using a soft pencil, ruler, and triangle, draw in your listed features in possible locations. Start each new design on a clean sheet of tracing paper.

DESIGN GUIDELINES

All the elements for one-room living need to be considered together. When planning your space, bear the following points in mind.

❶ CREATE SPACE by careful analysis of requirements and clever planning, and through the use of multipurpose furniture and movable or folding units.

❷ MAXIMIZE LIGHT by preserving and increasing any sources of natural light with the installation of full-height or full-width mirrors and by enlarging windows.

❸ USE VERTICAL HEIGHT to create a raised sleeping or working platform, providing useful storage space underneath.

❹ REDUCE CLUTTER by careful planning of plumbing and electrical services, working to box them in as much as possible.

❺ EASE OF ACCESS is essential, so make sure that you leave enough space for doors to open and for unimpeded movement around the furniture and fixtures.

REJECTED PLANS

The complexity of planning for one-room living varies according to how much space is available. If the room is large, each living function can be comfortably separated; if it is very small, the goal must be not simply to fit everything in, but to do so in a way that conveys an impression of spaciousness.

POOR USE OF SPACE ▽
The cooking area is in the darkest part of the room, with very little counter space, and the table, seating only two, is in the opposite corner. There is no room for easy chairs.

BATHROOM DOOR
When the bed is down, there is barely room to open the bathroom door.

SHOWER AND BOILER
The shower cubicle blocks access to the boiler, and their close proximity is potentially hazardous.

BLOCKED DOORWAYS ▽
The futon offers comfortable seating but, when it is opened out, access to the bathroom is blocked. The wardrobe door cannot be fully opened, as the kitchen unit is too close.

CLOSET
Insufficient room between closet and kitchen unit impedes access.

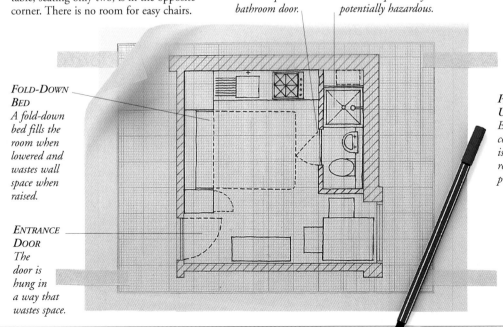

FOLD-DOWN BED
A fold-down bed fills the room when lowered and wastes wall space when raised.

ENTRANCE DOOR
The door is hung in a way that wastes space.

PENINSULAR UNIT
Even with a corner sink, there is still not enough room for food preparation.

DOOR BADLY HUNG
The door opens against the kitchen cabinet crowding the entrance.

Successful Plan

With clever planning, and despite limited room, the basic elements for one-room living can be arranged to create a workable space that is neither cramped nor uncomfortable.

Sink
A tiny sink has been recessed into the wall of the shower area.

Bathroom Door
To save space, a sliding door, with a glazed panel to let in light, has been fitted.

Two-Burner Stovetop
A practical two-burner stovetop, built in to the kitchen counter, provides adequate cooking facilities.

Boiler
The boiler, behind easily removable shelves, can now be accessed for servicing.

Wall of Storage
Every inch of wall space is occupied by cabinets or shelves, which, in turn, can be filled with boxes and files.

Mirror-Fronted Doors
An illusion of space is created in the bathroom by light reflected from the mirrors.

Narrow Armoire
A narrow, full-height armoire is fitted between the bathroom and the sofabed.

Sofabed
Maximizing space, the sofabed shares space with a drop-down table: when one is down, the other is up.

Door Rehung
The door has been rehung, giving a clear entrance and a direct, open view out of the window.

Drop-Down Table
A hinged, drop-down table provides a dining table to seat five, or a good-sized work surface.

◁ **Spacious Feel**
A sense of spaciousness has been created by tucking the bathroom into the corner with the plumbing, and making the two major pieces of furniture – the sofabed and the table – share the main living area.

Shaker Peg-Rack
A peg-rack makes the most of wall space for hanging folded chairs, coats, and umbrellas, as well as other hanging storage.

Full-Height Mirror
Hung next to the window, a mirror lengthens the interior space and bounces light back into the room.

Futon
The futon provides flexible seating and a bed, but abuts the kitchen cabinet when unfolded.

Poor Access to Different Areas ▽
In this scheme, a studio couch frees space, but this is spoiled by the dominant position of the shower unit, and by the kitchen cabinets blocking light from the only window. There is room for only a low, movable table for dining purposes.

Cramped Toilet
The toilet, fitted below the boiler, is cramped, and there is no room for a sink.

Shower Cubicle
A feeling of claustrophobia is created by the too-dominant shower.

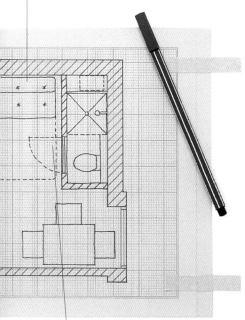
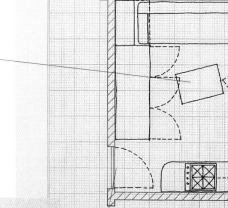

Dining Area
Armoire and bathroom doors open into the center, leaving room for only a low, movable table for dining.

Access to Bathroom
With the futon extended, access to the bathroom is blocked. The boiler is still dangerously close.

Entrance Door
The door has been rehung, but the entrance is now visually blocked by kitchen cabinets.

Blocked Window
The only natural light source is partly obscured by kitchen cabinets and corner shelving.

PLANNING DETAIL

CHOOSING THE INTERIOR FURNISHINGS AND FINISHES is, for many people, the most enjoyable part of planning a room. But, when making your choice of furniture, wall coverings, flooring, and lighting, be realistic about your budget and time, as well as bearing in mind our Design Guidelines for studio living (*see p. 78.*)

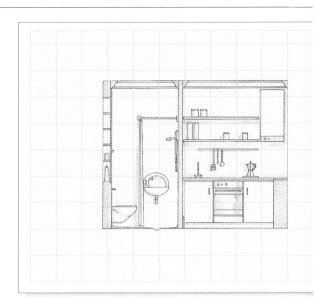

◁ LIBRARY OF IDEAS
As part of the planning process, collect pictures from magazines and catalogs that appeal to you, building them up into a library of ideas that will help you clarify your preferences for furnishing your home.

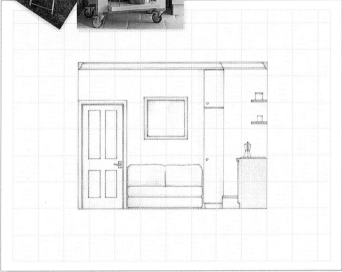

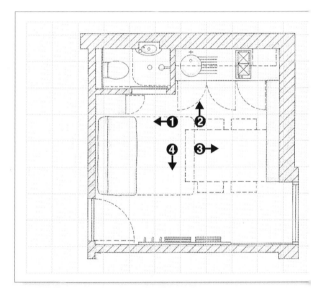

△ ❶ SLEEPING AND RELAXING AREA
As there is no room for a bedroom, a sofabed provides for both sleeping and relaxing, leaving the central space clear. A floor-to-ceiling closet fills the gap between the sofabed and the washing area, while a mirror on the wall above the sofabed reflects light from the window opposite.

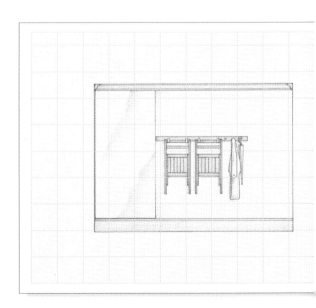

❹ USING WALL SPACE ▷
Space is created by clearing the floor and hanging folding chairs, coats, and umbrellas on a Shaker peg-rack. A full-height mirror alongside the window increases the apparent size of the interior, as well as improving the lighting level in the room.

◁ COLLECT CATALOGS
Send for catalogs of products advertised in magazines, and visit hardware and interior design stores to pick up literature on the furniture and equipment you like.

COLOR SAMPLES ▷
When collecting samples of your favorite materials, colors, and finishes, ask for fairly large pieces: it is hard to visualize the final effect from small samples.

◁ ❷ PLUMBED-IN SERVICES
The bathroom and kitchen have been lined up along one wall with existing plumbing. A curtain can be pulled around the low-level shower to protect the rest of the toilet space, and a small sink is set into the wall. The kitchen has two burners, an oven, a utensil rack, and shelving.

WHAT NEXT?

■ If your plan simply involves moving and installing ready-made cabinets and appliances, find a recommended carpenter or cabinetmaker to help you install these to your design.

■ If you want to move plumbing and wiring, to construct a raised level, or to change the interior structure, contact an architect who will take on the responsibility for dealing with the relevant authorities, obtaining planning permission, and making sure that building regulations are followed.

■ Before starting work, draw up a schedule in conjunction with everybody involved. The usual sequence of events is as follows: structural alterations; wiring and plumbing; laying floots; installing cabinets; then final electrical, plumbing, and decoration work.

■ Check that the delivery dates for appliances, cabinets, and materials will meet your agreed work schedule.

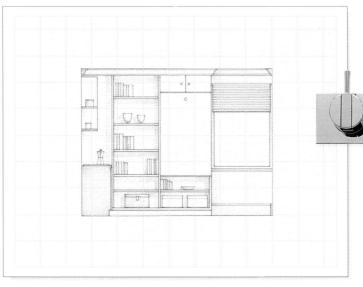

△ FIXTURES
Look for space-saving fixtures that combine several functions, such as this immaculately designed one-handle mixer faucet with integral soap magnet.

▷ FLOOR PLAN
A bird's-eye view of this compact interior shows the elements arranged around the walls, with the sofabed and drop-down table sharing the central space.

△ ❸ BUILT-IN STORAGE CABINETS
Built-in cabinets are the most efficient way of using space, and they help keep clutter at bay. Behind the drop-down table is a wall of shelves, while the rest of the unit is fitted with more shelves. The traditional casement window has been replaced by a one-pane pivot window for maximum natural light.

FLOORING AND FINISHES ▷
Check the composition when choosing materials. The difference between natural and synthetic materials is now very subtle, and many synthetics offer better and more durable properties than their natural counterparts.

BUDGET TIPS

■ Once you are satisfied with your basic plan, calculate the cost of buying the furniture, appliances, fixtures, and materials that you have chosen. Obtain estimates from architects, builders, plumbers, electricians, and decorators. If the total cost is beyond your budget, look carefully at each item to see where savings can be made.

■ When costing your design, remember that quality pays when it comes to finishes, both in terms of durability and personal comfort. Beware the false economy of bargains.

USEFUL ADDRESSES

The following directory of useful names and addresses will help you find the storage items needed for every part of your home.

FURNITURE AND ACCENTS

ADVANCED FURNITURE OUTFITTERS
PO Box 741
Bryan, OH 43506
Tel: (800) 501-1110
Fax: (800) 501-2220
Furniture for home offices, entertainment centers, kitchens, bedrooms, and more. Mail and phone orders.

ALINO NETWORK USA/DALIA KITCHEN DESIGNS
1 Design Center Place
643 Boston Design Center
Boston, MA 02210
Tel: (617) 482-2566
Tel: (617) 482-5592
Fax: (617) 482-2744
Dining nooks and cabinets designed to save space. Call for dealer referrals and phone orders.

ANDERSON BEDROOM ORGANIZER
Tel: (800) 782-4825
Underbed dressers with up to sixteen drawers. Call and request catalog $55.

ARROYO DESIGN
224 North Fourth Avenue
Tuscon, AZ 85705
Tel: (602) 884-1012
Furniture custom sized and designed. Call for catalog; phone orders.

BALLARD DESIGNS
1670 DeFoor Avenue NW
Atlanta, GA 30318-7528
Tel: (800) 367-2775
Accessories for the home. Call for catalog.

BED, BATH, AND BEYOND
Tel: (800) GO BEYOND
Accessories for the home, including linens and small appliances. Call for store locations.

BRUETON
145-68 228th Street
Springfield Gardens, NY 11413
Tel: (800) 221-6783
Mirrors, sconces, and other accessories. Call for product information and retail stores.

CRATE & BARREL
Tel: (888) 249-4158
Home furnishings and equipment. Call for catalog and store locations.

CURTIS CO.
40 East 19th Street
New York, NY 10003
Tel: (212) 673-5353
Fax: (212) 979-9713
Bookcases, Murphy beds, computer stations, and other home furnishings. Phone orders.

DAVIS FURNITURE INDUSTRIES, INC.
02401 S. College Drive
High Point, NC 27261-2065
Tel: (910) 889-2009
Fax: (910) 889-0031
Bar stools and stacking chairs. Call for the locations of retailers.

THE DESIGN STORE AT THE DOOR STORE
599 Lexington Avenue
New York, NY 10022
Tel: (800) 433-4071
Furniture for every room, including sofabeds, flip-top tables, etc. Call for catalogs and store locations.

EASTERN BUTCHER BLOCK
25 Eagle Street
Providence, RI 02908
Tel: (401) 273-6330
Fax: (401) 274-1811
Oak, maple, and ash furniture. Call for catalog.

EDDIE BAUER
PO Box 97000
Redmond, WA 98073-9700
Tel: (800) 789-1386
Fax: (206) 869-4629
Furniture and accessories for the home. Call for catalog and retail stores.

GOLDEN OLDIES
PO Box 541625
Flushing, NY 11354
Tel: (800) 435-0547
Specialists in antique armoires, many refurbished to hold televisions, stereos, and other electronics.

GRANGE
200 Lexington Avenue
New York, NY 10016
Tel: (800) Grange-1
Furniture for every room. Call for catalog and phone orders.

GREEN FURNITURE COMPANY
267 Commercial Street
Portland, ME 04101
Tel: (800) 853-4234
Email: wwwinfo@Greendesigns.com
Call to request home furnishings catalog.

IKEA
Tel: (800) 434-4532 Regional
Tel: (410) 931-8940 East Coast
Tel: (818) 912-1199 West Coast
Furniture for every room. Phone orders; call for catalog.

JENNIFER CONVERTIBLES
Tel: (800) JENNIFER
Nationwide chain of sofabed stores; call for store locations.

JOHN KELLY FURNITURE DESIGN
Tel: (800) 291-1301
Email: JKFurnDsgn@aol.com
Furniture for every room, including folding screens, day beds, and tall, slender dressers. Call for brochure; phone orders.

LIGNE ROSET USA
200 Lexington Avenue
New York, NY 10016
Tel: (800) 297-6738
Sofabeds and other furniture. Call for catalog; phone and mail orders.

L.L. BEAN
Freeport, ME 04033-0001
Tel: (800) 341-4341
Fax: (207) 552-3080
*Call to request home
furnishings catalog.*

MARK SALES CO., INC.
151-20 88th Street
Suite 2G
Queens, NY 11414
Tel: (718) 835-9319
*Imported, unfinished wood
furniture. Call for catalog.*

**MAXWELL FINE
FURNITURE**
715 Liberty Street
Bedford, VA 24523
Tel: (800) 686-1844
*Hardwood furniture, including folding screens,
daybeds, and slim dressers made to fit into tight
spaces. Call for catalog and phone orders.*

METAMORPHOSIS
1347 Spring Street
Atlanta, GA 30309
Tel: (800) 700-9141
Fax: (404) 378-8141
*Ergonomic computer furniture.
Mail and phone orders.*

MURPHY BED COMPANY, INC.
42 Central Avenue
Farmingdale, NY 11735
Tel: (800) 845-2337
Fax: (516) 420-4337
*Manufacturers of folding wall beds.
Phone and fax orders; call for catalog.*

NEIMAN MARCUS
PO Box 650589
Dallas, TX 75265-0589
Tel: (800) 825-8000
*Home furnishings and accessories.
Call for catalog.*

NEW WEST
211 Big Horn Avenue
Cody, WY 82414
Tel: (800) 853-4234
*Custom western-style furnishings, including
bunkbeds, daybeds, and sofabeds.
Call for catalog; mail and phone orders.*

O' VALE
Tel: (908) 933-0437
Fax: (908) 933-0848
*Modern furniture, scaled-down
for small spaces.
Call for catalog and phoneorders.*

PIER 1 IMPORTS
Tel: (800) 477-4371
*Furniture, lamps,
decorative imports.
Call for retail store locations.*

POLIFORM USA
150 East 58th Street
New York, NY 10155
Tel: (212) 421-1220
*Custom-made beds, wall units,
and closet fittings.
Call for consultation.*

POTTERY BARN
Mail Order Department
PO Box 7044
San Francisco, CA 94120-7044
Tel: (800) 922-5507
*Furniture and accessories.
Phone and mail orders; call for catalog
and store locations.*

**ROSS-SIMON'S GIFT & HOME
COLLECTION**
9 Ross Simon's Drive
Cranston, RI 02920
Tel: (800) 458-4545
*Mirrors, china, home furnishings, and more.
Catalog and mail order service available.*

SAM FLAX ART AND DESIGN
12 West 20th Street
New York, NY 10011
Tel: (212) 620-3038
*Computer armoires, shelving,
and other furniture.
Phone orders.*

SPIEGEL, INC.
PO Box 182-555
Columbus, OH 43218-2555
Tel: (800) 345-4500
Tel: (800) 645-7467
Fax: (800) 422-6697
*Home furnishings.
Call for catalog and
store locations.*

S.Q.A.
10201 Adams Street
Holland, MI 49424
Tel: (800) 253-2733
*Stacking chairs.
Call for product information and local retailers.*

THOMASVILLE HOME FURNISHINGS
PO Box 339
Thomasville, NC 27361
Tel: (800) 584-3829
*Living room and bedroom furniture.
Call for catalog and retail stores.*

THIS END UP
PO Box 2020
Richmond, VA 23218-2020
Tel: (800) 627-5161
Fax: (804) 321-9883
*Furniture for every room, including wall systems,
apartment-sized sofas, and shelving units.
Call for catalog.*

WORKBENCH
180 Pulaski Street
Bayonne, NJ 07002
Tel: (800) 656-7891
*Bookshelves, storage units, and other furniture.
Call for catalog and store locations.*

STORAGE

THE ANTIQUE HARDWARE STORE
1C Mathews Court
Hilton Head Island, SC 29926
Tel: (800) 422-9982
*Medicine cabinets, umbrella stands, and other
storage related items. Call for catalog.*

**BENJAMIN MOORE
PAINTS**
51 Chestnut Ridge Road
Montvale, NJ 07645
Tel: (800) 826-2623
Tel: (888) BEN MOORE
*Call for store locations,
distributors, and product
information.*

CALIFORNIA CLOSETS
Corporate Headquarters
1700 Montgomery Street
San Francisco, CA 94111
Tel: (800) 873-4264
Tel: (800) 325-6738
Tel: (415) 433-9999
Custom closets.
Call for brochure and store locations.

CLOSETTEC
555 Providence Highway
Norwood, MA 02062
Tel: (617) 769-9997
Custom closets and storage systems.
Call for product information and
local retailers.

THE CONTAINER STORE
2000 Valwood Parkway
Dallas, TX 752340-8880
Tel: (800) 733-3532
Fax: (800) 786-5858
A complete line of storage items.
Call for catalog; phone and mail orders.

DELTA ACCESS USA
8182 Maryland Avenue
Suite 806
Clayton, MT 63105
Tel: (800) 327-3589
Storage systems. Call for catalog.

EXPOSURES
PO Box 3615
Oshkosh, WI 54903
Tel: (800) 222-4947.
Shelves, ledges, boxes, and other
storage accessories. Call for catalog;
phone and mail orders.

FEENY MANUFACTURING CO.
PO Box 191
Muncie, IN 47308
Tel: (800) 899-6535
Organizers, grooming racks, cosmetic
drawers, hampers, and recycling bins
designed to fit inside cabinets.
Call for local store locations.

HOLD EVERYTHING
3250 Van Ness Avenue
San Francisco, CA 91409
Tel: (800) 421-2264
Storage items designed to create space:
shoe racks, specialty hangers, wall mounts,
bathroom and closet organizers, shelves,
drawers. Call for catalogs and store locations.

LIBERTY HARDWARE
MANUFACTURING CORPORATION
314 South Chimney Rock Road
Greensboro, NC 27409
Tel: (800) 542-3789
Hooks, lifts, and racks made to conceal,
as well as hanging baskets and other decorative
storage items. Call for retail stores.

MARKUS CORPORATION
10 Wheeling Avenue
Woburn, MA 01801
Tel: (617) 932-9444
Gadget rack and kitchen tools
designed by Philippe Stark.
Call for product information
and local retailers.

REV-A-SHELF
2409 Plantside Drive
Jeffersontown, KY 40299
Tel: (800) 388-2681
Kitchen and bathroom drawer organizers.

RUBBERMAID
1147 Akron Road
Wooster, OH 44691
Tel: (330) 264-6464
Storage products for every room.
Call for retail stores.

SCHULTE CORPORATION
12115 Ellington Court
Cincinnati, OH 45239
Tel: (800) 669-3269
Fax: (513) 247-3389
Closet and home storage systems.

SPACEMAKERS CLOSET INTERIORS
600 Wilie Road
Marietta, GA 30067
Tel: (770) 952-3455
Custom-crafted closet interiors.
Call for a local store.

STAPLES
Tel: (800) 333-3330
Hooks, racks, shelves, and
other storage items.
Call for catalog; phone orders.

APPLIANCES

ACME KITCHENETTES
CORPORATION
PO Box 348
Hudson, NY 12534
Tel: (800) 322-4191
Tel: (518) 828-4011
Under-the-counter refrigerators
and compact kitchen units.
Call for store locations
and mail-order service.

CERVITOR KITCHENS, INC.
10775 Lower Azusa Road
Elmonte, CA 91731
Tel: (800) 523-2666
All-in-one compact kitchen units
specially designed for small spaces.

DWYER PRODUCTS
418 North Calumet Avenue
Michigan City, IN 46360
Tel: (800) 348-8508
Tel: (219) 874-2823
Compact kitchen units; phone orders.

GE APPLIANCES
General Electric
AP 35-Room 1007B
Appliance Park
Louisville, KY 40225
Tel: (800) 626-2000
Tel: (502) 452-4557
Manufacturers of compact dishwashers,
cooktops, and refrigerators.

MAYTAG
240 Edwards Street
Cleveland, TN 37311
Tel: (800) JENN AIR
Wall ovens. Call for product information
and retail stores.

RICHLUND SALES
75695 Highway 1053
Kentwood, LA 70444
Tel: (504) 229-4922
Fax: (504) 229-4956
Compact dishwashers, compact
washer-dryers. Call for catalog
and phone orders.

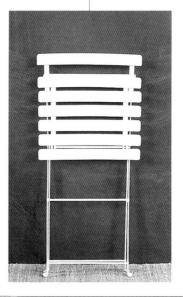

WALLS AND WINDOWS

AMERICAN DISCOUNT WALL AND WINDOW COVERINGS
1411 Fifth Avenue
Pittsburgh, PA 15219
Tel: (800) 777-2737
Fax (412) 232-4683
Custom upholstery and decorator fabrics.
Phone, fax, and mail orders.

BENJAMIN MOORE PAINTS
Tel: (800) 826-2623
Tel: (888) BEN MOORE
Call for store locations, distributors, and product information.

HANCOCK'S
3841 Hinkleville Road
Paducah, KY 42001
Tel: (800) 845-8723
Fax: (502) 442-2164
Decorator fabric; call for catalog.
Phone, fax, and mail orders.

HUNTER-DOUGLAS
2 Park Way South
Upper Saddle River, NJ 07458
Tel: (800) 327-2030
Tel: (800) 937-7895
Shades, blinds, vertical and horizontal dividers. Call for retail store locations.

NATIONAL BLIND AND WALLPAPER FACTORY
400 Galleria #400
Southfield, MI 48034
Tel: (800) 477-8000
Wallpaper and blinds.
Phone and mail orders.

LIGHTING

BRASS LIGHT GALLERY
131 South 1st Street
Milwaukee, WI 53204
Tel: (800) 243-9595
Fax: (414) 271-7755
Brass sconces and table lamps.
Call for catalogs.

BULBMAN
630 Sunshine Lane
Reno, NV 89502
Tel: (800) 648-1163
Fax: (800) 548-6216
Wholesale lighting distributors.
Call for catalogs and mail orders.

GOLDEN VALLEY LIGHTING
274 Eastchester Drive
Suite #117A
High Point, NC 27262
Tel: (800) 735-3377
Fax: (800) 760-6678
Wholesale sconces, ceiling fixtures, and more. Mail, phone, and fax orders; call for catalog.

MAIN LAMP/LAMP WAREHOUSE
1073 39th Street
Brooklyn, NY 11219
Tel: (718) 438-8500
Fax: (718) 438-6836
A wide array of lamps and lighting fixtures.
Mail and phone orders.

SUPPLIES AND HARDWARE

HOME DEPOT
Corporate Offices
2727 Paces Ferry Road
Atlanta, GA 30339
Tel: (800) 553-3199
Nationwide chain of home-supply stores. Call for catalog, product information, and addresses of retail outlets.

TOOL HAUZ
122 East Grove Street
Middleboro, MA 02346-1288
Tel: (800) 533-6135
Tel: (508) 946-4800
Fax: (508) 947-7050
Tools and hardware.
Mail, phone, and fax orders.

TOOLS ON SALE
Seven Corners
Hardware, Inc.
216 W. Seventh Sreet
St. Paul, MN 55102
Tel: (800) 328-0457
Phone and mail orders; catalog available.

MISCELLANEOUS

BROAN MANUFACTURING CO.
926 West State Street
Hartford, WI 53027
Tel: (800) 548-0790
Built-in hair dryers.
Call for store locations.

DUPONT CORIAN
Barley Mill Plaza
PO Box 80012
Wilmington, DE 19880-0012
Tel: (800) 4-CORIAN
Ready-to-install shower-stall kits.
Call for product information and references to retailers.

GUSA, INC.
250 South Executive Drive
Edgewood, NY 11717
Tel: (800) 842-4872
Sconces, mirrors, and a full line of bathroom shelving, including grooming racks and towel rack. Call for local retailers.

HIDE-AWAY IRONING BOARDS
5563 104th East Avenue
Tulsa, OK 74146
Tel: (800) 759-4766
Tel: (918) 493-6566
Fax: (918) 494-6866
Ironing boards that store against closet interiors or walls. Call for retail stores.

IRON-A-WAY
220 West Jackson Avenue
Morton, IL 61550
Tel: (309) 266-7232
Fold-away and built-in ironing boards, built-in scales. Call for phone orders and referrals to local stores.

PUTNAM ROLLING LADDER CO. INC.
32 Howard Street
New York, NY 10013
Tel: (212) 226-5147
Fax: (212) 941-1836
Custom rolling ladders.
Fax and phone orders.

SONY
Tel: (800) 222-SONY
Manufacturers of "mini" entertainment and audio systems. Call for product information and local retailers.

TREASURE CHEST CUSTOM AQUARIA
12970 Old Forge Road
Waynesboro, PA 17268
Tel: (718) 762-4546
In-wall installation kits for aquariums and betta tubes (miniature desktop aquariums.)
Mail and phone orders.

INDEX

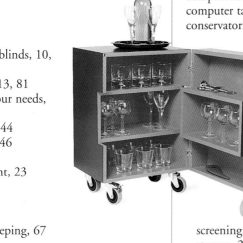

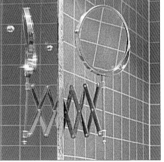

ACKNOWLEDGMENTS

AUTHOR'S ACKNOWLEDGMENTS

I would like to say a big thank you to everyone at DK for keeping me in line to work on this book at a major turning point in my life, and in particular to Irene Lyford, my editor, for her composure, to the creative book designer Ina Stradins, to Ally Ireson for inventive picture research, and to Charlotte Davies, the series editor, for her sensitivity; not forgetting my original editor, Sally Paxton, now in distant parts, who got the project up and running.

Many thanks also to those who allowed us to invade their homes, and to the talented photographer Jake Fitzjones and his inspired stylist partner Shani. She is so good at her job that the owner of a new one-room apartment photographed for the book bought the props she had chosen for the shoot.

A very special thanks also to Lois Love for all her leads, and especially to the architect Clifton Page for demonstrating that small spaces can be very pleasant to live in.

PUBLISHER'S ACKNOWLEDGMENTS

DK would like to thank: Ally Ireson for picture research; Robert Campbell for technical support; Hilary Bird for the index; Sharon Moore for design assistance; Sally Paxton and Murdo Culver for their work on the early stages of the project; Sacha Talbot-Dunn at Warner's Film & Location Transport for help with furniture moving; and Jim Thompson for help with a lighting crisis.

We would like to thank the architects whose plans appear in the book: Andrew Hanson and Nazar al-Sayigh of Circus Architects 66–7; Jason Cooper Architect 58–9; Seth Stein Architects 70–1; Simon Colebrook of the Douglas Stephen Partnership 62–3; Voon Yee Wong of VX Designs 54–5.

We are also grateful to Guy Greenfield Architects (7, 24–5tc, 34bl) and Clifton Page Architect (22c) for help with other locations.

We are indebted to the following people, who generously allowed us to photograph in their homes: Cheryl Bell, Jake and Shani Fitzjones, Rt. Hon. Nicholas Gage, Ian Hay, John Howells, Natalia Inclan, John Knights and Lesley Craig, Sue Macartney-Snape, Clifton Page, Voon Yee Wong.

We would also like to thank the following individuals and companies who lent us photographs and items for photography: Abet Ltd.; Aero 14tl, 22–3c; 23tc, 26br, 41c; Helen Allen 4br, 16tl, 22bl, 86t; Alouette Innovation Ltd. 21cl, 83b; Antique Baths of Ivybridge 33tl; Arc Linea 16bc, 25bc; Ariston 85b; Alouette Innovation Ltd. 21cl, 83b; Tomoko Azumi 21bl, 21bc, 21br, 35tr, 85t; Cheryl Bell 47bl; Belling Appliances Ltd. 25tr; James Bermudez 1, 30bl, 30bc, 34tr, 34–5c, 35tl, 82b, 88bl; Bisque 9r; But Furniture 40cl; Campbell & Young 45tr; Cato 40bc; China & Co. 44br; Crabtree Kitchens 26bl; Crucial Trading Ltd.; Dimplex 86; Divertimenti; Elizabethan Photographic/ Abet Limited 6tl; Susan Fairminer 46–7; Jonathan Field 38cl; 38–9bc; First Floor 44tr, 45tl, tc, bl, br; Fitzroy's Flower Workshop Ltd.; Robert Fleming Designs; Futon Company 20bc, 20br; Graham & Green; Habitat 3cl, 23br, 29br, 31tc, 46tr, 46tr, 46br, 47tl, 47tc, 47tr, 84b; Thomas Hall 21c, 21cr; Ian Hay 47bc; Heal's; The Holding Company 40br, 41tc; Simon Horn 35br; Ikea 10br, 15tl, 17br, 23tl, 35cr, 41tbc; Innovations 41tr; Key Industrial 31cr; The Kitchenware Company; John Knights 8bl, 8cl; Manhattan Loft Corporation 8tc; Meyer 24bl; Muji 20cr; Paperchase 31bc; Pivotelli 23cr; Poggenpohl 26bc, 27tr, 27br, 28bl, 36bc; Precious McBane 12l; Primrose & Primrose; Radiant Distribution 47br; Rainbow Carpets & Curtains Ltd. 45bc; Rembrandt Arts & Crafts; The Rug Warehouse; Scotts of Stow 24cl, 25cr; SCP; Winfried Scheuer-

Authentics 88tr; Simply Bathrooms 17tl, 33cr; John Strand 24bc; Strouds of London; N.V. Vasco 10cr; Tefal 37ct; Tenco 32bc; Viaduct 4bl, 11r; 15bl, 29tr, 31cl, 83t; Vola UK Ltd. 81cr; Whirlpool 37tr; Alison White 5br, 11tl, 87t, front jacket main image; Zanussi Ltd. 25br, 27tc.

Thanks also to Tim Head for permission to photograph his work of art "Levity," 47bc.

ARTWORK

David Ashby 22tr, 25bl, 31bc, 43bc. Richard Lee 3, 5cl, 5bl, 50c, 50–1c, 54c, 54–5c, 58tl, 58c, 62c, 62–3c, 66c, 66–7c, 70c, 70–71c, 77 (scale plans), 78–79 (floor plans), 80–81 (plans and elevations).

PHOTOGRAPHY

All photography by Jake Fitzjones, Andy Crawford, and Matthew Ward except: Peter Anderson 27cr, 27bc, 28tr, 76–77 (measuring your room); Avotakka/Camera Press 52tr; Richard Bryant/Arcaid (architect: Pierre D'Avoine) 73; Jeremy Cockayne/Arcaid (architect: Yann Weymouth) 72tl; Peter Cook/View (designer: Hugo Tugman Partnership) 57; Friedheim-Thomas/Elizabeth Whiting & Associates 60tl; Chris Gascoigne/ View (designer: Nick Hockley at Orms) 65, 72bc; Steve Gorton (front jacket main image); Graham Henderson/Elizabeth Whiting & Associates (designer: Sue Pitman) 60bl; Rodney Hyett/Elizabeth Whiting & Associates 52tl; Ray Main 44cl, 60–1, 69; Diana Miller 26tr; Nadia Mackenzie/ Elizabeth Whiting & Associates 68bl; Ian Parry/Abode 68–9; Alberto Piovano/Arcaid (architect: Kris Mys) 72bl; Spike Powell/ Elizabeth Whiting & Associates 13br; Roger Ressmeyer/© Corbis 6bl; Trevor Richards/ Abode 60tc; Paul Ryan/International Interiors (designer: Miki Astori) 52br; Paul Ryan/ International Interiors (designer: John Michael Ekeblad) 64tr; Paul Ryan/ International Interiors (designer: Kristina Ratia) 56tl; Fritz von der Schulenburg/The Interior Archive 41tl; Fritz von der Schulenburg/The Interior Archive (designer: Dot Spikings of Bare Foot Elegance) 53; Andreas v. Einsiedel/Elizabeth Whiting & Associates 68tl; Schöner Wohnen/ Camera Press 20tr, 38tr, 38cr; C Scott Frances/Esto (Corrine Calesso, Architect) 52bl; C Scott Frances/Esto (Walter Chatham, Architect) 42bl; C Scott Frances/Esto (Thomas Leeser, Architect) 64bl; Elizabeth Whiting & Associates 39br, 56bl, 56c, 64tl.

Every effort has been made to trace the copyright holders. We apologize for any unintentional omission and would be pleased to insert these in subsequent editions.

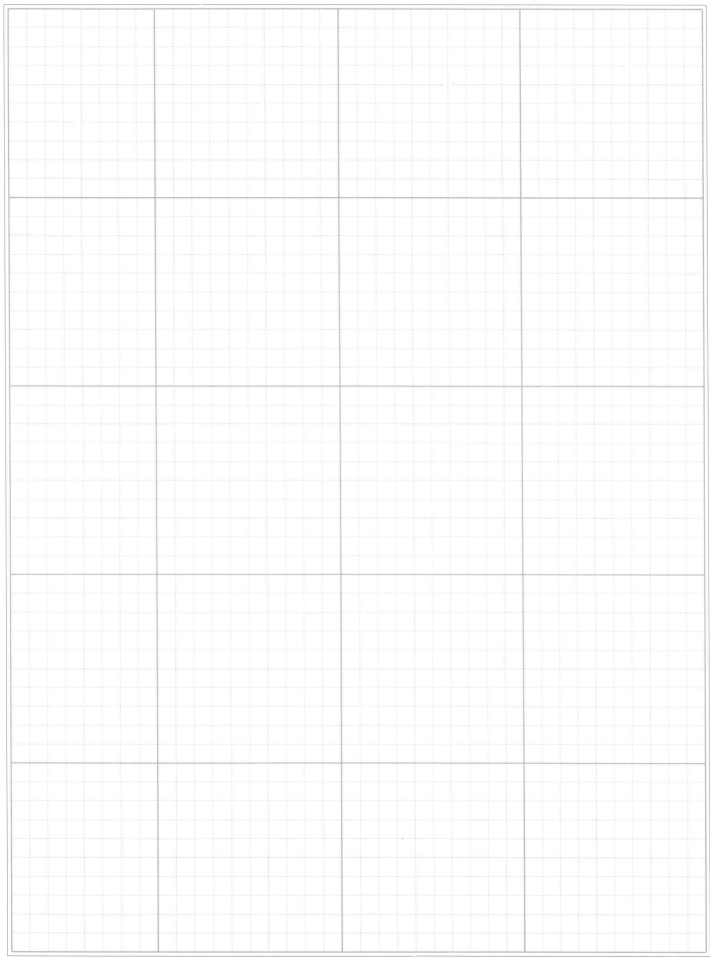

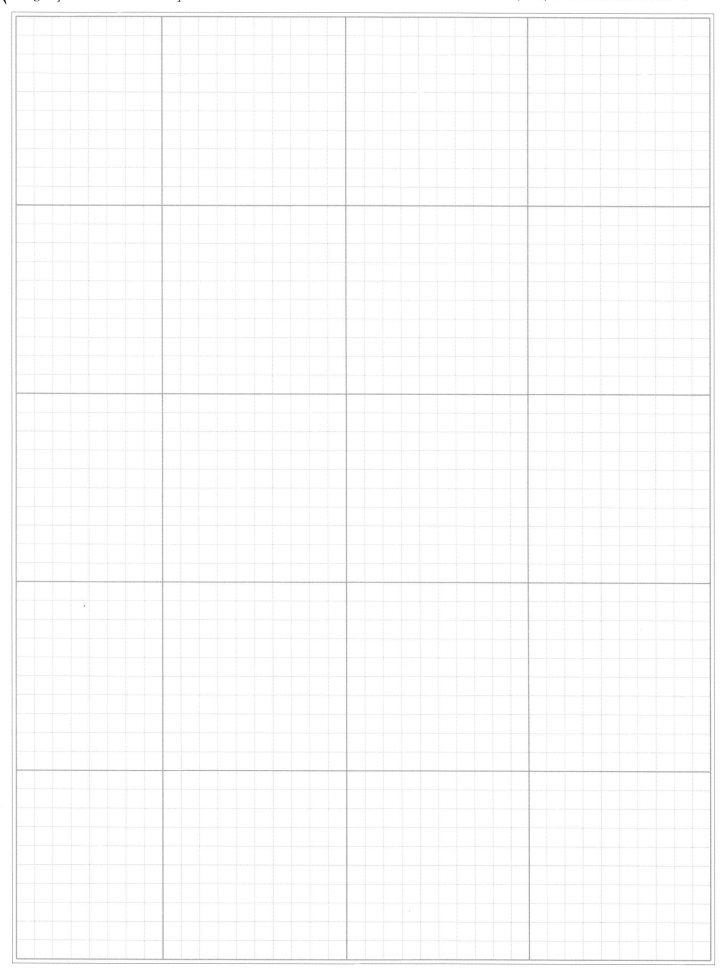

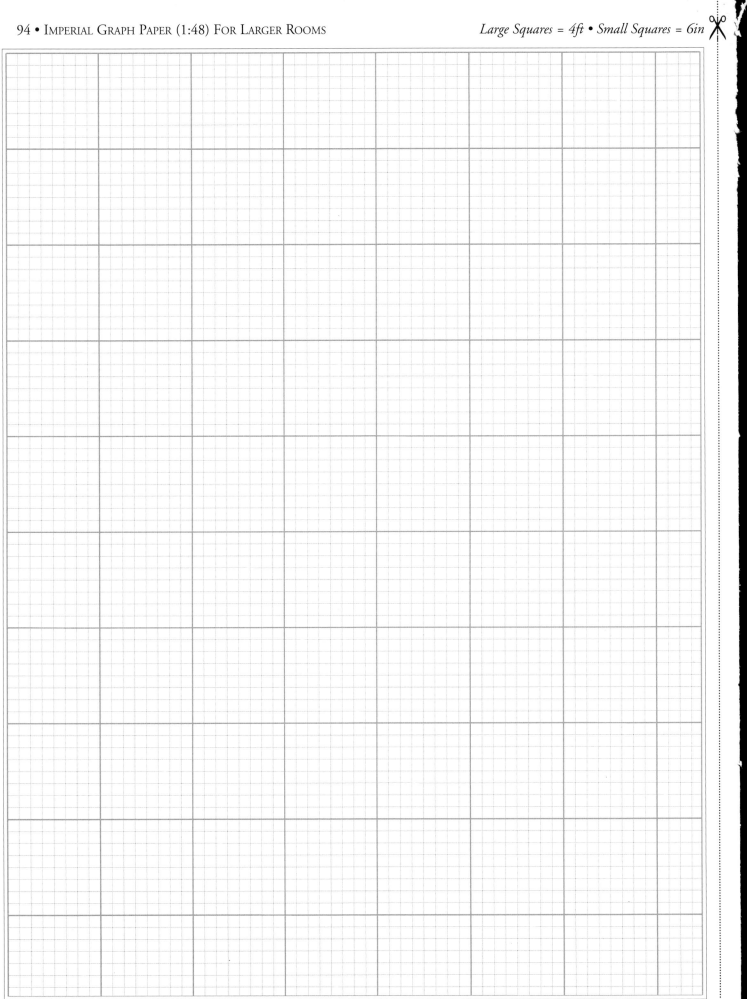

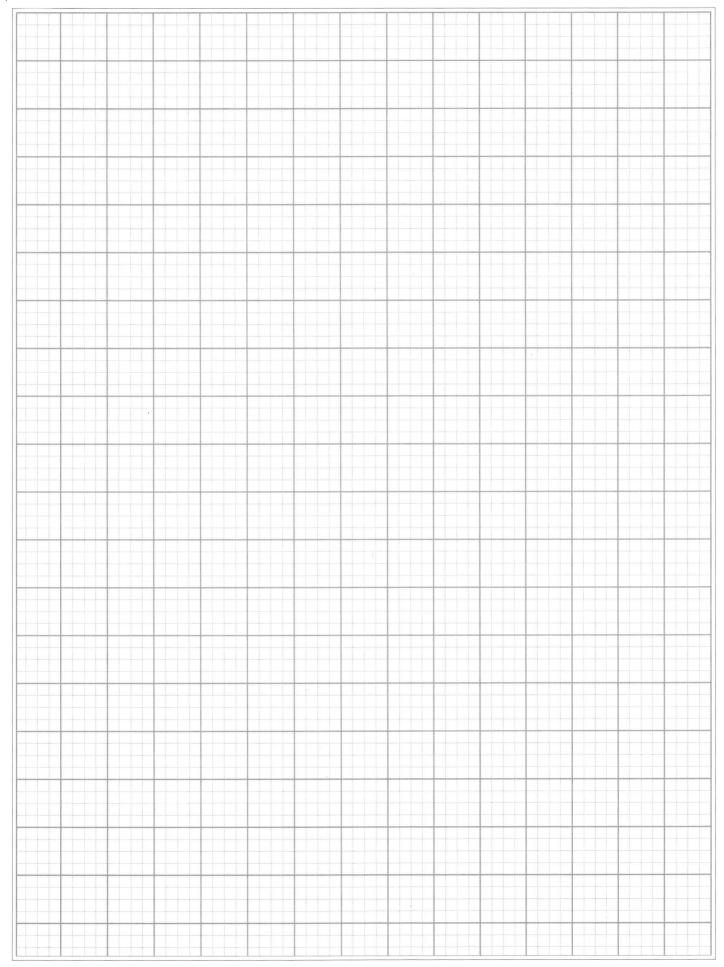

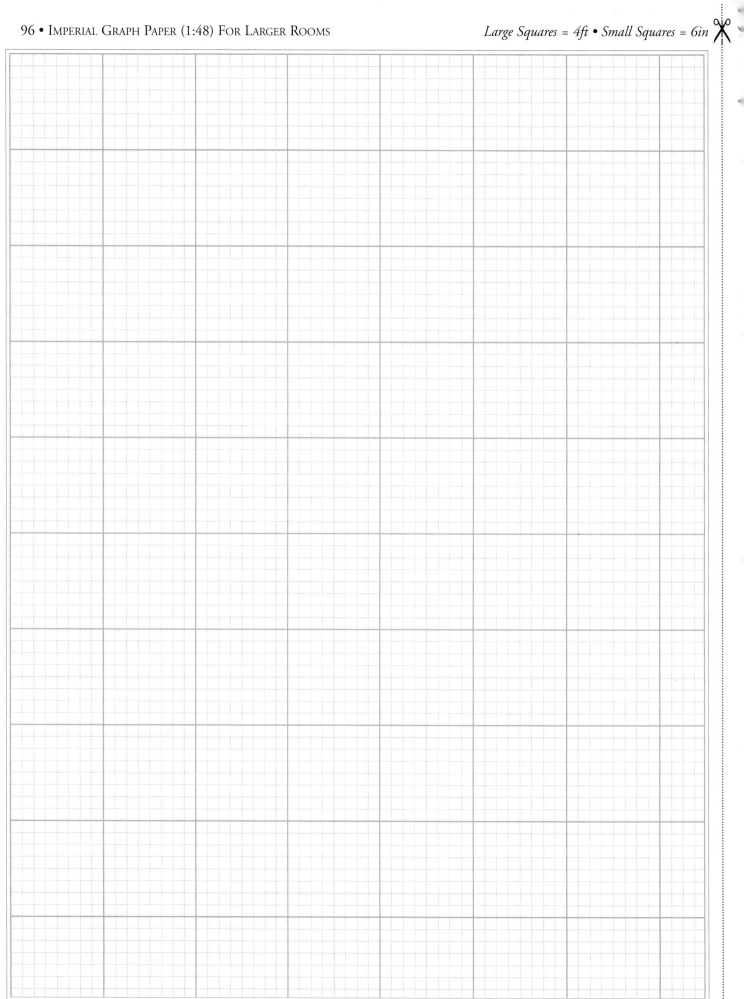

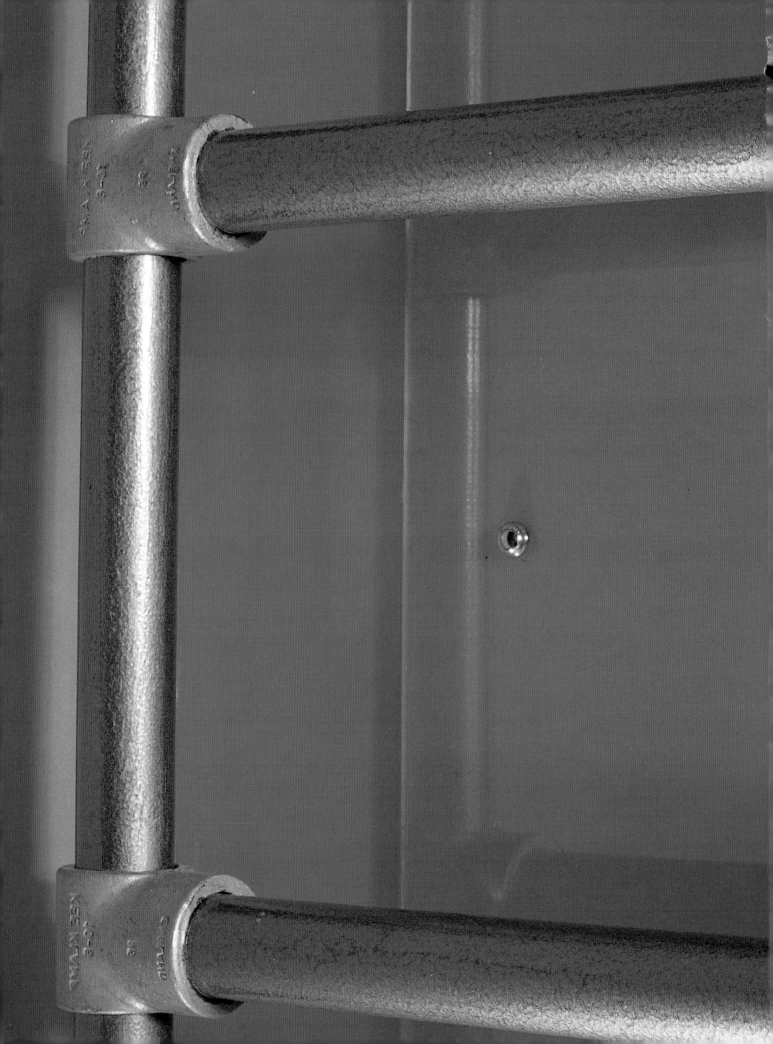